DISTORTED

How a Mother and Daughter Unraveled the Truth, the Lies, and the Realities of an Eating Disorder

Lorri Antosz Benson

Taryn Leigh Benson

Health Communications, Inc.
Deerfield Beach, Florida

www.hcibooks.com

Library of Congress Cataloging-in-Publication Data

Benson, Lorri Antosz.

    Distorted : how a mother and daughter unraveled the truth, the lies, and the realities of an eating disorder / Lorri Antosz Benson, Taryn Leigh Benson.

    p. cm.

    ISBN-13: 978-0-7573-0594-8 (trade paper)

    ISBN-10: 0-7573-0594-6 (trade paper)

    1. Benson, Taryn Leigh—Mental health.   2. Eating disorders in adolescence—Patients—United States—Biography.   3. Bulimia—Patients—United States—Biography.   I. Benson, Taryn Leigh.   II. Title.

RJ506.E18B46 2008

618.92'85260092—dc22

[B]

2007048399

Publisher: Health Communications, Inc.
              3201 S.W. 15th Street
              Deerfield Beach, FL 33442-8190

Cover design by Andrea Perrine Brower
Interior design and formatting by Lawna Patterson Oldfield

CONTENTS

To Our Family
Especially Steve, the best husband and father in the world

ACKNOWLEDGMENTS

We would both like to thank our agent, Stuart Krichevsky, and his staff for their patience, wisdom, and guidance throughout this project. Your hand-holding paid off! Thank you to Cathy Saypol, who, in spite of the passing of over a decade, jumped back into our professional friendship and got this book off the ground. Thanks to our insightful, caring, and intuitive editor, Allison Janse, and our friends at HCI, who have collaborated to make our ideas come alive.

Thank you to all the treatment teams that aided in Taryn's recovery, most especially Kit Corbett, who was always ready to listen and encourage. We appreciate our friends who helped us through the dark days, particularly Laurie Gregory who understood and walked the walk with Lorri, and Mariellen Bergman who jumped on an airplane for a girlfriend rescue mission. A big thank you to Floyd Poling, for all of the hours he spent bringing *Distorted* to the web.

Most importantly, we would like to express our gratitude to our family. To June and Leo Antosz, thank you for reading and re-reading and giving us much needed feedback. To Linda Smyth and Kim Wagner, thank you for your support and open ears. To Scott Barson, you have given inspiration and encouragement, and even more—thank you for always believing in us. Taylor and Halli, you lived through such sad and difficult times—thank you for your unconditional love and forgiveness. Finally, to Steve— you are such a blessing to both of us. You are always there, supporting our efforts and showing us in a million different ways how much you love us both. We are so lucky to have each and every one of you in our lives.

PROLOGUE

Sometimes an event occurs, a single event, and your life is changed forever. The funny thing is that you don't always have a clue when it happens. It doesn't have to be something inherently huge, although sometimes it is, and it doesn't always appear to have monumental impact at the time, although sometimes it does. It just happens. And your world changes. Completely.

An event like this occurred to me on February 16, 2003, when I walked in on my sixteen-year-old daughter making herself throw up.

It was a night like most others—trying to fit the busy lives of three girls and two parents into one schedule while making sure there was a little family time thrown in for good measure. Sixteen-year-old Taryn, our oldest, was cheering at a basketball game. With a little maneuvering, the rest of us—Taryn's almost fourteen-year-old sister, Taylor, her nine-year-old sister, Halli, and her dad and I—were all able to attend the game.

Afterward, we decided to go for dinner; Taryn chose the spot. She picked International House of Pancakes. Although we never ate there, we knew she and her friends frequented it, so we soon found ourselves enjoying platefuls of lingonberry, chocolate ⌐   o, and other assorted pancakes.

⌐   aned her plate and then helped Halli with hers. I ⌐   inking, *That's a switch,* since Taryn was usually more ⌐   ortions, salads, and healthy eating, like so many ⌐   s teenage girls were.

⌐   nced her departure, since she'd driven her own car⌐   the game, and Taylor jumped up, declaring, "I'll ride ⌐   ." Later, I would understand Taryn's irritation and pro⌐ st, but at that moment, we just cajoled her into taking her sister with her.

The rest of us headed home, just a few minutes after Taryn and Taylor. As I opened the garage door, I heard gagging sounds from the bathroom just inside. I walked the few steps to the closed door in slow motion. Although I knew what I was hearing, my brain couldn't reconcile the meaning immediately. *Who was it? Was she sick? Why the muffled gagging?*

I knocked. Long moments passed, waiting for something to happen, for something to be said. "I'm sick," came her quiet response to my silence outside the door. Click, click, click: the snapshots from our dinner started coming into focus, fast and furious. After a moment frozen in time, I reacted, shrieking, "What are you doing in there? Open this door!"

Normally, my husband and I are careful, thoughtful parents.

We don't yell; we explain, we reason. That night, my fist hit the door. "Open the door," I said, in a calmer, yet far more threatening voice. The door opened.

"What are you doing?" I repeated, knowing the answer, yet somehow hoping for a less horrible end to this scenario. Nothing. A blank stare, her eyes studying me for a clue. How much did I know? How much could I guess?

"I know what you're doing," I said, with conviction, because I did, very unfortunately, know what she was doing. As the former senior producer of a long-running talk show, I had done many shows on eating disorders, anorexia, and bulimia. "How long have you been doing this?"

This line of questioning continued until finally, when she ran out of excuses, Taryn started talking. "I haven't been doing it that long" and "I hardly ever do it." "It's just something I've tried," and "It's not a big deal." I listened, and in that moment, my relationship with my daughter changed forever, my trust in her crumbling.

When I insisted that she would have to talk to a therapist, she was incredulous. "Are you kidding?" she squealed. "Mom, you're making way more of this than it really is." But then, maybe too quickly, she acquiesced.

CHAPTER ONE

Once Upon a Time

You know the story. We were the lucky ones, the happy family: two parents crazy about each other, three great kids, a blessed life. We had just built a lovely home in a terrific neighborhood in a gorgeous Florida coastline city—nothing wrong with this picture.

I often told myself that if we just did everything right, if we gave our girls the right balance of love, respect, and discipline, we might get through the tough teen years without incident. Even so, there was a part of me deep inside that was waiting for the shoe to drop; a part that knew, someday, we'd have some big obstacle to face. After all, life is never perfect. I remember worrying something might happen to my husband, Steve, or one of the girls might have a terrible accident. Every now and then, I'd think, *It can't always be this great . . . something will happen . . . what will it be for us? We can't be this happy, this fortunate.*

I was right.

Until the moment of truth in the bathroom, I was completely blind to the seriousness of my daughter's outlook on life, and I had no clue that our challenges were already in progress. Up until that shocking February night, life with our family was better than we could ever have expected. Sure, there were the bouts of sibling rivalry, the messy bedrooms, the homework nagging, but nothing unique to us, and nothing to indicate that anything was out of the ordinary.

When people would roll their eyes and laughingly wish me luck when they heard I had three of the fairer sex, I didn't get nervous. I grew up as the middle child in a family of three girls, so having girls was very familiar. Plus, I don't scare that easily. At least, I didn't then.

Taryn was our oldest and a golden child in every way. She always wanted to do the right thing and was never any trouble. Looking back, there are moments that might have shed light on the problems she would later develop, but at the time, everything we experienced with Taryn, the baby and the growing child, seemed perfectly normal.

Monday-morning quarterbacking just doesn't really help, because at each step along the way, there was someone telling us we were in a normal phase. Later, when we were told of studies researching a possible connection between colic, tantrums, and similar behaviors to the development of eating disorders, we remembered moments from Taryn's childhood. But at the time, her doctor and my friends would just laugh, shake their heads and tell us the colic, the tantrums . . . this, too, would pass. And there's just as good a chance that they were right, and these incidents really were just a part of growing up.

My husband and I traded our high-powered New York jobs to move to Florida so that we could spend more time with our girls. He stepped down from his position on the Wall Street trading floor, and I left my job as senior producer of the long-running talk show *DONAHUE*. Taryn had just turned eight, Taylor was five and a half, and Halli was eighteen months. We chose that time thinking the girls were young enough to suffer no repercussions. We'll never know if we were wrong. Just before we moved, Taryn had tested into the gifted and talented group, so after settling her in her new school, we made arrangements to test her for the Florida equivalent, the Challenge Program.

To our surprise, she didn't get the required score. I remember being disappointed, since we'd been told the Challenge curriculum was as good as any private education. But the administrator reassured us, tossing around possible explanations such as "the move," or "new surroundings." She suggested Taryn finish out second grade and retest, which she did. This time, she was accepted into the program. No big deal. No big drama.

Could this have been the start of Taryn not feeling good enough, when she decided she had to work harder, do a little better than everyone else? Maybe. Maybe not. I noticed that with each passing grade in elementary school, Taryn seemed a little more shy, but I saw no reason to panic. At home, with her sisters, she was boisterous and confident. She would put on shows, dress up, and boss the other two around. No problem.

Then came middle school, which was rough for Taryn—a time of uncertainty, change, fear, and pressure, when young minds and egos are influenced to act and feel a certain way, whether they are ready or not. They are screamed at, by everything they see, hear, and read, to be older, act more sophisticated, and yes, to be thin, gorgeous, and (yikes!) sexy. At age twelve.

We tried to fight those influences with family time: church every Sunday and a strong Catholic foundation; sunsets on the beach every Friday, followed by our family dinner-out ritual. We monitored the movies, the TV, and the Internet. We rocked and read stories. We explained and reasoned. We did what we were supposed to do, and we didn't give in to every whim. I chose my battles, however. On subjects like contact lenses or shaving legs, I recognized the intense desire to fit in, and while innocence was lost and peer pressure seemed to come too soon, I understood and relented.

Taryn became more focused on trying to walk the walk and be in the "right" crowd. Her academics were perfect—always straight A's—but she yearned for popularity, and she didn't always feel successful. I remember many late-night talks while I scratched her back. I ached for her hurt feelings, her anguish, her tears. So I did what any mom would do.

I reassured her. Again, and again, and again. "You are so beautiful, Taryn. I know right now you hate your nose . . . can't stand your hair . . . feel fat . . . but only you see it this way. You're such a pretty girl . . . you have so much going for you . . . look at all the positive things. In a few years, you're not going to believe how gorgeous you are."

I was half-right. She still doesn't believe it.

And though she always seemed so hard on herself and would look at the glass of her social world as half empty, her behavior didn't seem that different from my friends' daughters or any of the other preteen girls.

During her freshman year in high school, everything seemed to come together for Taryn. She learned how to deal with her wild curls. The braces came off. And most important, she made the dance line, one of only four freshmen to do so. Suddenly, she was thrust right into the middle of the fun crowd. She had a boyfriend and plenty of invitations.

Steve and I shared in the enthusiasm of high school. Taryn was so busy and traveling right along the path we'd dreamed she would. She joined clubs, volunteered, continued with her straight A's, and danced at every football game. We never had to tell Taryn to do her homework or focus on schoolwork. Never. She knew what she had to do, and she did it. She was organized, made lists, accomplished projects on time. As the ultimate procrastinator, I admired so many of her wonderful traits. The only downside was that she put so much pressure on herself, like so many kids do today. In this competitive world, they have to be outstanding in so many ways. We had no clue how far Taryn took her perfectionism.

One day I was driving Taryn to her annual physical when she told me she thought she was anorexic. Kids say a lot of things, and I looked at her, wondering if she was trying to push my buttons, or if this was something more. There were no real signs of a problem. There had been the occasional offhand comment about dieting, but what teenage girl didn't talk about dieting? What woman didn't?

So when Taryn mentioned this to me, no warning bells went off, and I automatically went into maternal caution mode, reminding her how deadly eating disorders could be, and that they were serious. Later, at dinner, when I noticed she was polishing off an unusually large amount of food, still no bells went off in my head. Because there were no overt signs of trouble, no dots to connect, I casually remarked she didn't have to overdo it.

By the time I caught her throwing up in the bathroom, Taryn was in the middle of her sophomore year. At age sixteen, she'd given us a few moments of pause . . . some acting out over the summer, a couple of suspicious evenings, nothing too out of the realm of teenage normalcy. Since we spent our summers in Colorado, we blamed her lapses in judgment and social escapades on being away from her friends and hanging with a questionable crowd. Things would straighten out when we got home. And for the most part, they did. Taryn made the basketball cheerleading squad, remained on dance line, was a Big Sister mentor, had a job, was fifth in her class, in great shape, and beautiful.

In fact, whatever she decided to pursue, she made a plan and achieved it. In some ways, she seemed on top of the world. On the other hand, we still often talked into the night, and she still struggled with normal teenage angst. She looked at things negatively and sometimes even seemed depressed. Yet once again, it didn't seem all that strange.

I remember asking a friend with an older daughter about it, describing how Taryn would feel down even though her life seemed so great. "I know what you mean," she told me. "Katherine used to walk around like she lost her best friend." Yep. Just a normal phase. This, too, shall pass. Except it didn't. Although we didn't know it at the time, Taryn saw it all very differently.

I stared at my thirteen-year-old self in the mirror, brimming with thoughts of hate and self-loathing. I pinched my thighs . . . my stomach . . . my arms . . . every part of my body seemed to be in obscene excess. Settling down at my desk, I scribbled furiously in my brown notebook:

> Fat. Awful. Gross. I hate my body. I am going on a diet.
> I am going to lose 15 pounds and then I'll be perfect. Then maybe
> Drew will notice me. God, I wish he could understand how perfect
> we would be together. If only I wasn't so fat and ugly—ugh! I hate
> my body and myself.

Two years later I stared in the same mirror, pinching the same thighs . . . stomach . . . arms. Every part of my fifteen-year-old body was still disgustingly and overwhelmingly fat. But this time, I decided to do something about it.

I leaned over the toilet and jammed my first two fingers down my throat. I choked and gagged and vomited until my face and throat were both so swollen that I could hardly open my mouth. My jaw, which suffered from a bad case of TMJ, was popping in and out of place, and I was wavering from dizziness. But I still managed to smile. I absolutely loved this newfound feeling of emptiness.

I was positive, like almost every girl, that if I could lose ten pounds I would undergo this miraculous transformation and suddenly be the most popular and beautiful female on the planet. Since sixth grade I had experimented with endless crash diets and short-term weight-loss schemes. At the end of my freshman year of high school, about a month and a half before summer vacation, I started a new diet: fruits and veggies only.

It worked fabulously at first—I lost five pounds in two days and decided to continue until I went from my unacceptable 145 to 125 pounds.

Unfortunately, as most diets do, this one slowly stopped working. So I gradually had to cut more and more calories out of my diet. Meanwhile, one of my good friends, Kayleigh, also began to diet. Her diet was more of a fast, and it caught everyone's attention. People were talking about calling her parents, and everyone gossiped about how Kayleigh skipped lunch again. I secretly wished I could be her; I thought the negative attention was better than no attention at all.

I had never been popular in middle school. While I wasn't an outcast, I was a wallflower and kept to myself. When high school started

I vowed to change everything and tried as hard as I could to get attention from my peers. I did my hair differently, laid out in the sun on weekends to get a tan, and got a job so I could buy cool clothes. I had friends, but I was never satisfied. I wanted to be popular. I craved attention and I finally saw a way to get it. Even if people didn't notice my fasting, they would notice the eventual weight loss.

So the next day my diet turned into a fast. I sat in my ballet studio, sipping on a Diet Pepsi and waiting for class to begin, wondering how long I would have to hold out until someone noticed the fact that I, too, was starving! After three days of consuming nothing except diet sodas and water, I decided that I had had about enough. That afternoon, as my mom drove me, coincidentally, to my doctor's office for a physical, I told her that I thought I was anorexic.

Her reaction was not what I expected. Instead of a rush of concern and immediate scheduling of therapist appointments, I got a lecture on how my body was not a toy and how anorexia was a serious disease and not something to joke around about. I remember sitting in my doctor's office holding back my tears of embarrassment as he asked me, ironically, if I was eating all my fruits and vegetables.

That night my family and I went out to dinner and I decided to go all out and abandon my diet, which hadn't exactly had the desired effect anyway. My mother, watching me scarf down piece after piece of bread, pizza, an ice cream sundae, and more Dr. Pepper than most people could drink in a month, commented, "You know, after not eating anything for a few days, you should probably slow down a little."

Oh, shut up, I thought, with anger pulsating through my veins. *Like you even give a damn about my fasting anyway.*

The whole situation left me feeling humiliated and as fat as ever, the two things I was trying to avoid. I knew that a serious eating issue could get me the attention I craved, but I needed to do it right. It was a few months later when I started throwing up in another desperate attempt to be accepted.

I wasn't perfect, but until the year I turned fifteen I never got into very much trouble. This changed my first year of high school when I started experimenting with alcohol at a few parties during the school year and smoking cigarettes with friends when I claimed to be at the library. That summer, I lost my virginity to a guy that I knew from my job at a local coffee shop. I remember silently crying as he spent the fifteen-minute drive home making me swear over and over to never tell a soul so his girlfriend, whom I had never heard of, wouldn't find out. It was incredibly painful and a horribly humiliating experience, one that I vowed I would never get myself into again—but I didn't keep that promise.

The majority of my summer was spent in Steamboat Springs, Colorado, a beautiful little town surrounded by breathtaking mountains and a serious lack of things to do for any fifteen-year-old, much less one like me. I was always feeling depressed, constantly worrying about food and yo-yo dieting, and just wanted to go home. So I started making my own fun.

One night I took my thirteen-year-old sister with me to drink with some guy that I had met earlier in the day. I also tried smoking marijuana for the first time that night; my sister watched as I gasped and coughed and tried to look cool. As soon as we walked through the door of the condo, my parents clearly realized what had gone on.

After a single Smirnoff Ice, my sister could barely walk. I will always remember how my parents looked at each other with recognition that night and the knot I felt forming in my stomach. I could sense their fury. I was in trouble.

I eventually got ungrounded and tried to behave until we went home to Florida. My eating disorder continued to get worse; I started making myself throw up in September. I had read about bulimia and anorexia, and since at least four of my close friends were being treated for one or both of the disorders, I knew the basics. At first it was more of a quick fix; I only puked when I accidentally ate too much. An extra cookie or pancake would send me running for the toilet. It was the perfect solution to all of my weight-loss worries. It slowly started to take a different turn, however, when I discovered that I could eat twenty cookies and get rid of them just as easy as one.

Boys were a very big part of my life as I returned to school. I dated boys from the high school for a few months, but I slowly found myself becoming less interested in them and much more interested in someone completely unacceptable: a thirty-four-year-old guy named Nathan.

I was hosting at a popular restaurant in our hometown and he worked there. Since I was only sixteen, it was more than just a bad choice—I was legally off-limits. He also had a bit of a drug problem and was on probation.

It started out as nothing serious, just a casual "Hi" or "How's it going?" every now and then. But soon I started visiting him at his friend's house in a nearby town, usually with a few of my friends along. One night I sneaked out of my house and we went to another friend's house where we drank and smoked. That night Nathan and I kissed for the first time; it was a beautiful night with bright stars and the moon reflecting off the ocean.

Despite this new excitement, everything in my life was starting to become secondary to my obsession with food and my body. My bingeing and purging was becoming more frequent and the disease was getting deeper into my head. I started journaling everything about my diet; I recorded the amount of calories and grams of fat in everything I ate, the estimated amount of calories I burned during my daily exercise, and calculated my total caloric intake for each day. I spent hours scrutinizing my body and pinching my "problem areas" in front a mirror; I imagined my rumbling stomach sucking the fat from the places on my body I hated the most. I lay in bed praying I would wake up thinner.

The night my mother discovered my dirty secret was the best and worst night of my life. I was exposed. Naked. Vulnerable. And exactly where I wanted to be.

CHAPTER TWO

A Natural Disaster

February 2003

It was the best and worst night of my life. In the middle of a cough-gag-choke, the garage door slammed and I knew it was over. My "secret" bulimia, which had been going on for only a few short months, was exposed.

I think many people assume that bulimics and anorectics strive to hide their disorder and take pride in their big, guarded secret. This was definitely not the case with me. I lived for the manipulation; that was the fun part. Finding new and more creative ways to purge. Coming up with better excuses about why I really couldn't be there for yet another meal. And, of course, bullshitting through all the mornings when my family found all of their food miraculously gone. And getting away with it. Again.

Jealous of my friends who were "diagnosed," on medication, and seeing therapists, a big part of me was just waiting to be discovered.

13

I secretly craved the look on my mother's face as she burst through the bathroom door and cried out in that strained-whisper-scream voice she used whenever she didn't quite know what to do except be angry: "What do you think you are doing!?"

In the days that passed I watched my mom spend hours on the phone and computer—endless calls and e-mails trying to find the perfect therapist. I would casually slide by the office door, glancing in coyly like I didn't know what she was doing. I watched and listened, trying to gather every piece of information I could about how serious my mother considered my condition. This was very important in the manipulation. I was actually somewhat excited about starting therapy. I had never done anything like it before, and the few friends that I knew that had been through it had never really been eager to talk about it. I had this overwhelming desire to give an image of distress.

Even though a part of me wanted my parents to know about my bulimia, I certainly didn't want to stop bingeing and purging. Once they found out, this became much more difficult, so I began manipulating, lying, and taking extensive measures to hide my behavior. I turned on the shower or loud music to hide the noise of purging and sprayed cheap body spray around the bathroom to disguise the smell. I always made sure to wipe up the mess and would take off my shirt before throwing up so it wouldn't get stained from the vomit.

One night I came home from dance practice and found four or five different types of cookies on the kitchen counter. My parents were watching a movie in the next room. I shoved a handful down my throat and ran upstairs, hoping my parents wouldn't notice. I turned on the shower and lifted up the toilet seat as my mother burst through the door. I sat down on the floor—it was too late and another lecture was unavoidable.

I didn't sleep very much that night. Maybe I was in over my head. I was excited to see where this new road would take me, but I was also desperately afraid. I was enjoying the thrill of successful manipulation and felt a newfound sense of power over everyone around me; I was learning how to make people believe my lies, and it was amazing how easy it was. I also loved the way I looked. My whole life I had wanted to be just a few pounds smaller, and now I had found a way to thinness that allowed me to eat anything I wanted. A part of me was scared of how obsessive I was getting, but I also knew bulimia would give me everything I wanted. I would do anything to lose more weight.

The night in the bathroom with Taryn changed my life. Nothing was as I thought it was, and I was shaken, but not defeated. I was fairly certain that she was just experimenting with various behaviors and methods of losing weight, but I wasn't going to take any chances. I also wasn't going to let any time go by. Some kids try drugs; some get drunk every weekend. Seems my kid was obsessed with losing weight.

I didn't panic but had an awful tightening in my chest and a knot in my stomach, and I remember almost literally feeling the shoe drop on my "perfect" world. Even if this was a mere dalliance on Taryn's part, I couldn't understand how she could toy with harming her lovely body.

Over the years, I made a major effort to get healthy body messages across. "Our bodies need healthy fuel; exercise is important for our bodies; don't put things in your mouth that can hurt you," and so on. After consistently advocating making healthy choices, I just couldn't grasp why Taryn would willingly jam her finger down her throat. It was the first betrayal—the first realization that just because I delivered the information, it didn't mean that my children would be spared mistakes and their consequences.

My feelings went beyond disbelief. While I expected to face problems as a mom, this wasn't one of them. My job as a producer of *DONAHUE* had exposed me to plenty of episodes on eating disorders. I knew the hows and whys and what-not-to's. With three daughters, I knew this was a very real threat, and I had been determined to learn from those shows. No clean-plate club. Talk health, not diet. Focus on the inside, not the outside.

I knew that many times a trauma or family issue was at the root of an eating disorder. Because our family life seemed so normal and happy, it didn't occur to me that Taryn's mood swings and insecurities were anything but typical teen turbulence. And even when I caught her in the middle of a purge, I absolutely did not think full-blown "eating disorder."

I couldn't get a straight answer from Taryn. How long had this been going on? "Not long." What other things was she doing?

"Nothing, really." What made her start? "Everybody's doing it." Even though I always felt we had a close relationship, all of a sudden we were on different teams.

We went to our separate corners that night, and Steve and I settled into the trenches to mull over the discovery. While I certainly wasn't calling the cavalry or pressing 911, I knew in my heart this was a problem that needed addressing—and fast. Steve wasn't so sure.

"Do you really think this is such a big deal?" he asked. "She's probably just trying dumb stuff; being a typical teenager."

He thought perhaps we should just ignore it and see if the problem resolved itself. I'll never know if he was right, because *my* gut told me to waste no time. The frantic search for the right therapist was on. With my producer hat firmly on my head, I began researching our community for an eating disorder specialist.

I quickly discovered that it was a much smaller pool of experts than I had expected. We had a well-known eating disorders treatment facility in our town, and I felt sure that this resource could come to my rescue with all the information I needed. I was surprised to learn they did not treat adolescents and had no solid contacts for me.

Wow. I had my first feeling of being alone with my dilemma. Here we had what seemed to be a problem of increasing proportions in our society, and no local clearinghouse or go-to organization was available for a parent to get answers. It was time to start asking questions, networking, and interviewing.

I wanted someone who wasn't too "doctorish," who could relate to adolescents, and someone in whom Taryn might actually want to confide. I didn't mind that she might need to talk to another adult, although truth be told, there was probably a part of me, the part that always tried to be available for my kids, that resented that I wasn't enough. But, whatever. I needed someone to get through to my daughter.

After about two weeks of searching, I finally settled on Nina. Her name kept coming up with each contact I made. She'd actually been a therapist at the local eating disorder facility and had gone into private practice, specializing in eating disorders. She seemed like a great choice, but I told Taryn, "You can decide if you click with her. I want you to feel comfortable—I want you to like her. If you don't, I'll find someone else."

I didn't foresee this being a lengthy process. I figured Taryn would go to a few sessions, see that there were better ways to deal with her feelings, maybe get scared when the realities of an eating disorder were spelled out for her, get bored with having to sit in a room with a therapist, and everything would get back to normal.

CHAPTER THREE

False Hopes

February to March 2003

I was soon sent to see the first of many therapists—a very sweet woman with short, straight hair and long skirts. I tried my hardest to act as though I did NOT want to go and pretended to be extremely annoyed that I actually had to spend an hour of my ever-so-valuable time going to see this woman. Underneath, however, I could hardly contain my excitement—I had become my own little damsel in distress.

At first it was pretty exciting; an entire hour devoted to the discussion of *me* and how I felt—but it got old. Fast. I became sick and tired of mumbling "idontknow" and trying to figure out a way to sleep through the rest of the session. So I decided that I would continue with my eating disorder and try my best to ignore everything that went on during my appointments; I had learned the hard way to be careful what you wish for.

After a few months in therapy my eating disorder went from purging three or four times a week to every-other-day laxative abuse. I started taking three little pink pills every few nights, while everyone was sleeping. Three quickly turned to six, which turned to twelve, which eventually led to a whole box. Since I could buy these over the counter, no one knew my secret. The "laxative experience" entailed many early morning hours of excruciating cramping, puking, and, of course, "excreting." My weight went up and down depending on how much eating I was actually doing, but the laxatives were more of a safety net than anything else. I was too afraid of what would happen if I didn't take them.

I also started seeing Sara, a nutritionist at a local wellness center. She would weigh me and then go over meal plan after meal plan, setting up examples with the little plastic food items she kept in a basket by her desk. I liked her because she was young and seemed like she understood everything to a degree. Every week I presented fake meal plans—mostly filled in with a well-balanced diet—a little slip here, a purge or two there. Her sad smile made me wonder week after week if she believed anything, especially after weigh-ins where I was down nine pounds. At our last appointment she gave me a hug and turned back as she started to walk away.

"I understand it's hard, Taryn. I was in the same place you were once," she said, sadly. I remember wondering if she was sad because of me or sad that she wasn't sick anymore.

Since I was purging less, my parents began to back off a bit. I no longer noticed them looming around the bathroom corners as I excused myself after a meal. Puking was becoming increasingly less attractive, however, and I was experimenting with starving myself.

In February, just weeks after Taryn's cover was blown, I felt a brief period of relief. Taryn was in therapy once or twice a week, and I was in a holding pattern, waiting to see if my daughter would see the error of her ways and return to the carefree existence of a busy teenager.

That's not to say I simply handed the reins of worry over to Nina. I continued my search for information, surfing the Net, trying to find and talk to others in the same boat. That part wasn't easy. It became clear that this was a secret problem. Most people weren't all that excited about broadcasting the fact that their child was struggling with these issues. I heard from various sources that almost three-fourths of the high school dance line was involved in disordered eating, and I thought I'd be able to talk to other parents who were dealing with this. But when someone would suggest that this one or that one was rumored to be starving herself, throwing up, or dramatically dieting, I found that the parents either weren't aware of it, downplayed it as a phase, or simply denied it.

There weren't any outlets of information that told parents how they would feel, how to react, or how to reassure themselves. There were lots of firsthand accounts or medical websites, but for the life of me, I couldn't find out what I should do as a mother. I asked Nina if I could do a session or two with her to fill in any blanks I might have and to pick her brain about parenting strategies.

The first and second sessions went fine. They were informative, and I was finally able to ask about my role in getting Taryn back on track. "Should I treat her more gingerly, since clearly she's not feeling good about herself?" I asked. "Or perhaps I should take the tough love route." Nina explained that at this point, Steve and I needed to step back and try not to involve ourselves in our daughter's disorder. Our daughter's what? I just wasn't ready to accept that this was more than a passing phase. But okay, whatever. We would do what we were supposed to do.

Nina told me there was no quick fix. Taryn's recovery would take at least several months of therapy, and twice a week was better than once. In the back of my mind, I thought my brighter than bright daughter would figure this out and move on. It wouldn't take months. I started to worry that the cost could add up if we weren't careful. I sure didn't want Taryn getting used to what I thought was a luxury. Little did I know. It didn't take months. It took years.

The third session started to get on my nerves. Nina wanted to talk about my family history, my childhood, my parents. I didn't see the point, because I wanted my practical questions answered about Taryn: What should we be doing now? What else can we do? What can't we do? How does she really seem to you? And most important, is there really a problem here? Please tell me she's going to get past this and enjoy the rest of her high school years.

Instead, the questions about me continued. I knew many therapists liked to go back and explore childhood in therapy. The problem was that I wasn't the patient so I didn't see the point of going back and discovering that, as the middle child, I had a need to fix things, or that witnessing my parents fighting with my older sister made me determined to have a happy family life. Aside from Taryn throwing up her meals, I was happy.

Each time she would focus on me I'd answer and try to turn the session back to my frustrations in trying to open Taryn's eyes to the harm she was inflicting on herself. That's where I felt I needed help—someone to tell me what my role should be, because, as time went on, I became intuitively aware that she was still in trouble, and that knowledge terrified me.

While I wasn't seeing the outward signs of bulimia, Taryn was holding back, still not really communicating with us anymore. Now that we knew there were issues, other red flags began to wave in front of us. We noticed the skipped meals, the picky eating, the excuses. Especially the endless excuses.

"I'm late for work . . . I'll catch something to eat there."

"I already had dinner with my friends."

"I had a really late lunch after practice."

"I was too late to eat this morning."

"I'm a vegetarian now."

Although a mom might be a champion nutritionist and meal provider when her kids are young, once they're in high school, and especially once they're driving, all bets are off. You really lose your hold on whether they are eating their greens or subsisting on french fries and Cheetos. In our clan, I counted on "the family dinner" to ensure there was a little time together and at least one good meal a day. This works, unless a member of your family has an eating disorder. There were always reasons for her to miss meals; reasons that in another family would be par for the course. For us, every time we heard one of her excuses, we got a knot in our stomachs, because now, in addition to the threat of Taryn's purging, came the frightening awareness that she wasn't eating.

Steve and I often discussed the frustration of holding back our parental intuition. This became a recurring source of stress as we were repeatedly advised to hold our tongues when it came to Taryn's disordered behavior. We knew her weight was changing, but between her tall frame and layers of clothing, it was hard to know how many pounds had fallen off her body. We weren't allowed to ask.

For the most part, I tried to keep things in the family as normal as possible. There was no reason to get everyone freaked-out, especially when I was still trying to convince myself that we would quickly resolve the problem. I had no idea that instead, Taryn was seeking alternatives even darker and potentially more dangerous.

Anorexia was my goal. I would buy fashion magazines just to page through the endless pictures of skeleton-thin women, then I spent hours cutting out their pictures and arranging them in particular orders. I would group them based on what size I thought they wore, or just lay them out in a line in order from thin to thinnest. And sometimes I just looked at their faces, trying to decide who had just thrown up, which ones skipped lunch, who was snorting cocaine between shoots, and which ones had spent four hours on the treadmill that morning. I was obsessed with their skeletal bodies and craved that extreme thinness.

I wanted to be so skinny that people would stop on the street to stare at me. I needed to be that thin. Everything I ate was carefully weighed and measured to the exact calorie. I would freeze my yogurts for the morning so that I would eat them slower. The key was to eat everything as slow as you could so it had more time to digest. That way by the time you finished your exact 100-calorie meal, the hunger pains were not as bad as when you started.

In the beginning, most of the negative consequences traditionally associated with eating disorders were not apparent. I was hungry most of the time and had a little trouble sleeping, but otherwise I only noticed the positive sides: weight loss and attention. Later, when I went to a treatment center, tests and blood labs showed signs of multiple side effects, including a low platelet count, malnutrition, a low heartbeat, and a high pulse deficit. Although these issues would have caused severe problems later, I never noticed them in my day-to-day life, except for a little dizziness and blackouts when I stood up. Mentally, the problems were a little more noticeable; my anxiety was raging and I was very obsessed with eating and food.

I counted calories and grams of fat, every meal having to be a precise number of calories to be acceptable. Five hundred calories per meal, 300 calories, and eventually 100 calories: everything neat and tidy. If anything was just the slightest bit off, I would start drowning in waves of anxiety. It made perfect sense in my mind that one extra calorie or fat gram would make me blow up like a big balloon and all my efforts would be for nothing; it was incredibly frustrating.

As expected, I started dropping pounds during this time period, sending my 5'8" frame from 145 pounds down to 115. My parents watched with horror and my sisters sat like bystanders; I could see the fear in everyone's eyes. The starving and the purging seemed necessary to me. I was walking a tightrope, always teetering on the edge, knowing that if I fell off everything would have been for nothing.

I also started cutting a little, just a few nicks with a razor blade along the edge of my wrist—the brief physical pain allowed me an escape from the mental and emotional pain I was in constantly. It was similar to the way stubbing a toe momentarily relieves the pain of a terrible headache. For one tiny instant, you forget about your pulsing head and your whole focus is on the ache in your toe. Thus, through this twisted method of distraction, the heavy blanket of depression is lifted for just a moment as the blade pierces the skin—just long enough to see a glimmer of light from within the underworld.

CHAPTER FOUR

Off with the Mask

May to July 2003

It's funny how we humans instinctively "hope for the best," or believe that with one change or adjustment, everything will be solved. At this point, as Taryn's sophomore year drew to a close, I remember hoping that the summer and the change of scenery would bring good things.

Each June, we pack up the SUV and embark on a cross-country trek to Colorado. There my parents, sisters, their families, and ours descend upon our favorite condo cluster and spend the month hiking, fishing, boating, tubing, and hanging out together. We escape a summer of humidity in exchange for mountain air and family memories of grandparents, aunts, uncles, and cousins. I couldn't help but think that, in this environment, with only a caring family around her, Taryn might snap out of it.

Hard as it may be to believe, Steve and I actually enjoy our long car ride each summer. We stop to see friends and family along the way, and especially in this age of nonstop Frenetic Schedule-R-Us, we enjoy the time in the car with the girls, being together, playing games, watching movies, and talking. This summer, however, Taryn did not make the trip out with us. She was on a Jamaican mission with our church youth group, and she flew out to join us, after returning from Jamaica, with a one-night stopover at home. We weren't thrilled to have her home alone overnight, but it was only for about twelve hours. We told her the trusty neighbors were alerted, but we believed in her to do the right thing—plus we figured she'd be exhausted from her travel.

It's difficult to describe how I felt during the time Taryn was in Jamaica. I was worried about her, and I was a little hopeful for her. I knew she would be sleeping, breathing, and eating—especially eating—with her group. She would have very little, if any, time alone, I thought. If she was starving herself, or purging, surely her roommates or chaperones would notice. Perhaps witnessing abject poverty might show her how blessed her life was. And this was a different group from her dance line friends, and I thought maybe, just maybe, she might come back with a different point of view.

On the other hand, a week on her own might give her the break from our watchful eyes that she was seeking. My mind jumped back and forth, between hope and fear, and wait—could it be?—a little seed of relief, of respite, from the constant worry, the constant nagging worry that had been yanking my chain since February.

Because, if truth be told, it had gotten worse. She had now

been in therapy for three months. Although she went to see Nina willingly, I wasn't getting the feeling she was making much headway with Taryn. Things had definitely changed. Before the discovery in the bathroom, we really had no clue that Taryn was anything but an average teenager with ups and downs, highs and lows. Once we unearthed the truth, we became startlingly aware that some of what she felt, thought, and did was far from normal. It almost seemed like she wanted to be darkly abnormal.

I remember changing the bedskirt on her bed one day, and while adjusting it, I found a box under her bed. It was not your average box. This one scared the hell out of me. The top of the box, which was black and grey, was covered with pictures of skeletal-looking girls, cigarettes, and booze bottles. It was shocking, dark, and depressing. I was afraid to look inside but was surprised to see a bright, cheerful interior exuding happiness and girlish fun.

Across the top was written, "It's My Life." I just sat there, stunned and silent, the gloomy part completely obliterating the positive part. All I could think was, *She must be smoking, she must be drinking, and oh Lord, she's still deep into this screwed-up eating, must-be-thin mentality.* I tried to talk to her about it later, probing gently about what the box meant, but she waved it off as a kind of therapy project. I saw it as proof that she was keeping some deep, dark secrets, and the tension that came from waking up each day, knowing trouble was brewing, continued to grow.

So the idea of letting down my guard was tempting; of

spending days thinking of something else or not worrying. I would never admit how nice that oh-so-subtle relaxing of my shoulders and stomach felt; that would be a betrayal of my role as a mother. It would be a long time before I would realize it was okay to take a breather from wondering if Taryn was living or dying a little more that day.

However small that unacknowledged reprieve was, it was only to last until she stumbled off the airport shuttle from Denver, exhausted and still thin. Within a couple of days, my fears were back, my maternal instincts blasting warnings with a vengeance.

It was during this period that the turning point happened for Steve and me—the point that changed everything in our lives. The situation went from a teenage girl's turbulent adolescence to a full-blown crisis. And it came about because I did something I never thought I would do.

Sophomore year ended quickly. I was still attempting to diet; however, my frequent binges kept my weight fluctuating around 125—which was still on the thin side of my 5'8" frame. I remember bringing leftover salad to school in a plastic bag and watching all my friends stare as I calmly ate it with a fork as if there was nothing strange about eating a half a cup of soggy lettuce out of a sandwich bag. I took my AP exams running solely on Diet Dr. Pepper, caffeine pills, and an occasional cup of black coffee from Starbucks on my way to school. To this day I am shocked that I still passed.

I was still seeing Nathan a lot. He had been arrested for a violation of probation and went to jail for ten days. He was fired from the restaurant, but we kept in touch over the phone and about once or twice every other week I would sneak out of my house and we would drink and smoke cigarettes until dawn, when he'd drop me off down the street from my house. I loved everything about the relationship; it was so wrong that it felt right. Once the summer began I started to go to his house two or three times a week. I would claim to be running errands or going to the mall with friends and would make sure to be consistent with the story when my parents called my cell phone during the day.

We started sleeping together at the beginning of the summer. We would spend the day at the beach, drinking Dr. Pepper and rum or cheap beer and laughing with his friends. Then we would head back to his house and have sex and kiss good-bye and I would head home. He used to comment on how I would never eat a single morsel of food—even though I claimed to have a mammoth appetite and that I ate TONS at home (which was somewhat accurate). I remember him touching his thumb and middle finger around my upper arm and rubbing his hands along my protruding hip bones and ribs and whispering, "You're getting so thin, Taryn." I just laughed it off.

"No," I would smile. "I've always been this thin. I have a great metabolism. I eat tons, really I do!"

One morning, after a particularly disturbing fight with my best friend, I woke up early and spent the day on my lanai making a box. The bottom part of the box was covered in bright tissue paper and filled with pictures of laughing girls, beaches, and makeup. The top half, in contrast, was covered in gray tissue paper that I sponge-painted black and filled with pictures of desperately thin waifs, cigarettes, alcohol bottles, and the headlines from diet ads. I thought of the bottom of the box as representing what my life should be, and the top half a picture of what it actually was. I cut out magazine letters and used them to write "It's My Life" on the top of it. My mother found it a week later and flipped.

This was the beginning of my poetry phase as well. I lived with such intense emotion pumping through my brain all the time, and it lifted the burden slightly when I wrote it down on paper. I would sit in the back of my church curled up in my American Eagle football sweatshirt writing the depressing stanzas that still knot up my stomach when I read them now.

Lost. Confused. Alone.

WHICH WAY IS UP?
WHY DO I ALWAYS CHOOSE DOWN?
I CAUTIOUSLY STEP
ON SHAKY GROUND.
BLAZING THE TRAIL
WEARING A BLINDFOLD.
I WISH I COULD LEAD
AND SHOW OTHERS THE WAY,
BUT HOW CAN I MOVE
WITH THESE SHACKLES AND CHAINS?
MY HEAD HURTS
MY HEART ACHES.
MY SOUL SCREAMS IN PAIN.

BUT THERE IS NO ESCAPE.
I AM A FREE PRISONER,
A CAPTIVE OF MY OWN HAND.
I CRY TEARS OF BLOOD
ON THIS JOURNEY TO NOWHERE.

I went to Jamaica again that summer with my youth group, including my friend Jaime. She knew about all my food issues and, having had an eating disorder herself, knew a lot of the signs. We stayed in a convent, which, as expected, didn't have the greatest plumbing system, so purging was very difficult. I tried to eat as little as I could manage—mostly fresh fruits and an occasional fish, but it was never little enough. However, due to all the exercise I was getting from working outside all day, I lost four pounds.

The flight home seemed to last forever. Off the plane and finally alone, I was desperate. I stopped at the store on my way home to grab some binge food. My family had already left for Colorado, so I had one night alone in my house, and then I would fly out to meet them the next morning. I knew this would be a perfect opportunity to spend the night at Nathan's, but I needed to binge first. Ice cream, toast, and half a chocolate cake later, I drove to his place to spend the night smoking cigarettes and drinking with him, his roommate, and some other people. I finally went to bed around 3:00 or 4:00 and lay awake in his bed listening to Bob Marley play on the radio until 5:15 when my cell phone alarm went off. Before I left, I said good-bye, not knowing that this would be our last good-bye. He put his arms around me and said, "No, you're not going anywhere."

"Nate, I have to go! I'm going to miss my flight."

"So? Just stay here and live with me."

"No, I have to leave."

"You won't come back. I know that you won't. You'll just leave and never come back."

"Nathan! Yes, I will! Just let me go so I can catch my flight! I'll call you when we get back into town," and with that, I got up and made the drive home for the last time.

Granted, he would have never physically forced me to stay. He knew what the relationship was as well as I did—a fling of dangerous proportions. And he was also living in a completely different world than I was. He was an adult, no matter how much I didn't want to believe it, and he lived in a world that I didn't belong in yet.

I came home twenty minutes before both Kayleigh and Jaime picked me up to drive me to the airport. Laughing and telling them about my evening, I could tell through their forced giggles that they knew there was something very wrong about my relationship. I hugged them good-bye and gave them the rest of my binge food that I didn't have time to finish.

I scribbled madly in my blue journal on the airplane, unable to sleep as my Bistro Bag lay under my seat—uneaten. I prayed over and over the whole flight that my parents would never find out about my night.

In the end, however, someone completely unexpected would betray me.

CHAPTER FIVE

Blind Exposure

July 2003

I noticed that every now and then, Taryn would pull out a blue spiral notebook and scribble something in it. Sometimes I would knock on her door and enter, just as she was tucking the notebook down beside her. If she seemed anxious or upset about something, she would disappear and I'd find her writing away in that same blue journal.

As the days passed, and my anxiety level rose, my natural impulses kicked in and told me something was in that notebook—something that could potentially unlock the mystery of what was happening to my daughter. But could I actually invade her privacy like that? I had a strong respect for a person's confidential thoughts and writings, and never in a million years did I ever think I'd snoop in her journal.

But I did. I remember waking up one gorgeous Colorado morning, just a short time after Taryn had arrived. I woke up, feeling the morning chill and breathing in the luscious, cool air, and for just a moment, all was well in the world. Then, it all came back in an oppressive rush. I lay in bed, thinking about my ultra-thin daughter with her dangerous secrets, and I agonized over the idea that the answers could be as clear as that mountain morning, if I was ready to lower myself to that next, desperate level.

I was. As Steve awakened, I looked him in the eyes. "I'm thinking of reading Taryn's journal," I confessed.

He rolled over on his back, contemplating the idea, wondering about the repercussions. "I'm not sure if we need to go to those lengths," he finally offered.

"I'm not sure either," I answered, "but I'm afraid not to." My daughter seemed to be falling down a hole, and I felt like I was losing my grip on her hand. I felt compelled to do whatever I could to at least slow her descent, if not stop it. We sat in our bed and talked and, in the end, decided to do it.

The morning got started as usual. My sister's twins came knocking on the door to rouse the clan, and after some horseplay and rustling around in the kitchen, Taylor and Halli ran off with them. Taryn announced she was going to walk down to Starbucks. This was my chance. I gave Steve one more glance and sneaked into Taryn's room to begin the clandestine mission.

As I held the notebook in my hands and read her handwriting, I wondered if I was reading her journal or a piece of fiction. Was this a character she had made up? Was she writing a novel?

She was a good writer—maybe she was writing a novel. Maybe she was inventing a person she could vicariously live through on paper. But soon my naive maybes were replaced with an agony that is hard to describe. There were too many details I recognized. Too many answers to unasked questions I kept in my head. This was my daughter, and yet I had no idea who this person was.

The bingeing, the purging, the starving, the torture she felt about food, her weight, herself. While it was horrible to read, I had expected there would be some revelations about her struggles with eating. The rest blindsided me.

Oh Lord, Taryn is smoking, I thought. *How could she do that, after all we've told her?* Each new disclosure brought another wave of shock and horror as I realized just how bad the situation was. *And drinking!* I continued reading. *Omigosh, she's smoking pot!* and then, the real bomb exploded. *Oh no, oh no, oh no.* I ran from the room, notebook in hand. "Steve, she's had sex," I sobbed to him, "with some grown man who works with her— some sick pervert—and she was with him the night before she came here!"

My gentle husband's face grew hard and grim as he grabbed the journal and read the details—more than any parent wants to know, and more betrayal than either of us could ever dream we would feel. We'd done everything in our power to give our kids the best kind of upbringing. We'd given up plenty to give them a family-based childhood. We'd done our part. How could this happen?

I could understand if some trauma had occurred in her life. Or if Steve and I were never home. Or if she didn't feel loved or needed. Or . . . good grief, the list was endless. But we had tried so hard! We gave it our best effort. It just wasn't . . . fair. Yet how many times had I told the girls, "Life isn't fair." I now had to learn my own lesson.

The hardest thing to get past, however, was the feeling that God and the universe had let me down. I had done what I was supposed to do, and yet, here we were.

I must have shed a million tears. By noon, my eyes were swollen and I was sick to my stomach. We had a family outing planned with friends, and I knew there was no way I could make it through an afternoon of fun and casual conversation. We concocted a story about a mysterious, sudden flu, and I spent the afternoon in bed. I don't remember ever in my life spending a day in bed because of sadness. We needed a plan.

Over the next few days, Steve and I spent hours discussing the situation and formulating our next steps. We felt like a mix between method actors and private detectives. While Taryn had spent the last months manipulating us, now we were the manipulators. We never let on to Taryn that we knew anything, even while we copied the journal in case we needed evidence for the police back home. Steve was going back to Florida to catch up on some work, and while there, he was going to investigate this man, research the statutory rape laws, and attempt to get as much information as possible. My job was to see what I could get from Taryn without disclosing what I knew. The more I could get from her, the less risk that she'd find out I'd read her journal. I felt sure the discovery of that invasion of privacy would destroy our relationship and any hope of open lines of communication.

When Steve was leaving, I was filled with dread over my "assignment." I was being left alone to keep our family life as upbeat and carefree as usual so the other girls wouldn't suspect anything. As the days passed, so did my anger, shock, and anguish. The knowledge may have flattened me, but the discovery gave me an equal playing field. I wasn't the patsy anymore. Now when I asked her questions, I already knew the truth.

During this time, I had several lengthy phone sessions with Nina. I told her about the journal, and she helped us figure out the best way to deal with the information. She brought up the idea of inpatient therapy and mentioned one program that offered a weeklong mother/daughter retreat. I wasn't convinced. Perhaps I was a little overwhelmed with the suggestion that she might have a full-fledged eating disorder, the kind that couldn't be cured in a therapist's chair, along with everything else we now had on our plate. If we could get to the bottom of all these other issues, maybe the bizarre eating would taper off on its own.

I couldn't deny, however, that Taryn's eating, or lack thereof, was becoming a major problem. We would go to the store and scour the "Greenwise" and vegetarian sections, searching for food and sources of protein that she would eat, since she was now strictly avoiding meat. Our church held a nutritional seminar for families that Taryn, Taylor, and I attended. I was hoping

they would absorb the healthy eating message without my utter-
ing a word. Of course, Taryn, with her obsessive focus on food,
already knew much of the information. Like most girls with
eating disorders, she was knowledgeable, but powerless to stop
the destruction.

Under the circumstances, Taryn and I actually enjoyed each
other's company. She is a witty, clever girl, and fun to be with,
and we took walks and hikes together, always talking. I began
steering the conversations in the directions I needed to go, so
the stories Steve and I weaved during our long phone conversations would be believable. It was of utmost importance that she
not know the source of our information. At times I'd wonder, *Is
this really what parenting turns into—staying one step ahead with
manufactured alibis?* Our "sting" operation was planned, and
when Steve returned, we put it into motion.

I arrived in the afternoon at the complex in
Steamboat Springs where we would spend our
summer. My whole family was there welcoming me (my parents'
smiles a relieving sign that they were oblivious to my previous night's
activities) as I climbed out of the shuttle that had taken my sleeping
self the three hours from the Denver airport.

This vacation started extremely well from my perspective. Besides the occasional grumble from my parents about my not eating enough, everything was pretty nice. I read every book I could find about eating disorders and spent most of my time alone in my room, reading or writing in my journal. If I had to come out, I made sure I would be exercising so I would at least feel good about burning calories.

My mother and I would take long walks every day along the Yampa River or through mountain trails and talk about anorexia and dieting and our own opinions on the media's effects on women. However, these talks soon went from this place, where I was entirely comfortable to an area that made my stomach twist in all sorts of knots.

My mother spent one walk telling me how I could tell her anything and how sex was a sacred and beautiful thing that should be saved for love and/or marriage. I smiled and nodded and told her how I absolutely 100 percent agreed with her. About three days later she told me that she had gotten "a feeling" that I had had sex from our previous conversation. With my stomach in my throat, I stumbled through my response.

"Well, um, I guess so."

"Okay, Bill Clinton!" she exclaimed as I tried to keep my eyes focused on the flowers in the botanical garden we were passing through.

"Why would you say that?"

"Well, did you or didn't you? It's a pretty concrete question."

"Well . . . yes."

"With who?!?" I refused to tell her who and tried to act as remorseful as I could through my anger about the whole situation. I knew she hadn't just "gotten a feeling," and I wanted to know how she found out and who told her. I hated more than anything when my parents would lie to me about where they got their information, so I was determined to find out who let the cat out of the bag. I was old enough to know how my parents dealt with problems. My parents were a team, an indestructible team, and I had learned quickly that I couldn't just play one off the other. I had to face them head on. But I also knew my mother's secret weapon in finding out information about me. She knew my younger sister Taylor always knew my secrets, and usually she was too naive to realize our parents had just made her rat me out. They would come up with stories about how they already knew everything, but I always knew it was Taylor.

This time was different, though. I went to Taylor that night and sat on her bed, wondering if I should use the "I won't be mad, but . . ." technique or just start screaming.

"Tay, look, I need you to tell me something. Remember how I told you about how I had sex?" I looked for the horror in her face of knowing she had accidentally given me away again. My mother would usually tell her that she already knew something about me and ask for more details, and by the time I was confronting Taylor, she knew what was really going on.

"Yes," she replied hesitantly. I already knew by the look on her face it hadn't been her this time, but I wanted to double-check.

"You didn't say anything to Mom or Dad, did you?" I asked, watching her expression turn from confusion to hurt.

"I promised I wouldn't, Taryn! I swear I didn't say anything! Why do you always think I did something? It's not ALWAYS my fault!" she cried, big tears streaming down her cheeks. I felt no remorse, though. I got up immediately and left—I was furiously angry and didn't want to say anything offensive to the only innocent party . . . my only ally.

I wrote in the journal again . . . more and more. I thought maybe if I wrote everything out, the answer would come to me. It remained a mystery, though. I just couldn't figure out how they knew anything at all.

A week later my mother confronted me about how she knew that I had spent the night out the evening before I left for Colorado. She refused to tell me how she knew, only that she absolutely knew for sure. I assumed that my neighbors had ratted me out, but I wondered why it took so long for them to call and tell my parents. I was utterly confused about how my parents had happened upon this jackpot of information.

When my father came back into town, my parents took me on a long drive through the mountains and told me that they knew about my relationship with Nathan. They said that when my dad had stopped at the restaurant where I worked to pick up my check, one of the other employees had told him. I knew that this was absolute bullshit because no one else in the restaurant knew about it. So they said considering the fact that they knew that I had spent the night out and their newfound knowledge that I had this relationship with a man over eighteen years my senior, it was assumed that I had spent the night with him.

I was in complete shock at all of this. Lost about what to say, I just sat quietly in the backseat as my dad asked me if I wanted to press charges. When we finally got back to the condo, I locked myself in my room and scribbled in my blue notebook, the one thing I had found to bring me comfort on this vacation which had become extremely stressful.

Meanwhile, my eating situation continued to get worse. I was barely eating, and I was losing weight at a record pace. My parents and I fought about every piece of food I did or did not put into my mouth, and it was getting unbearable. I was sick of them bothering me, and they were falling apart from watching my daily self-destruction. My mother started sending away for brochures from inpatient centers, which I agreed to mostly because I didn't think I could live at home much longer. We analyzed treatment center after treatment center, making pro and con lists and diagrams. I stared at endless pamphlets, assuming that I wouldn't belong—I couldn't see how desperate my situation had become. The fact that something like inpatient treatment was even an option was a complete shock to me. I knew my bingeing and purging wasn't normal, but I wasn't so far gone that I had to be sent away. I wasn't that sick.

Although many of the conversations Taryn and I shared over that summer were part of the intentional setup Steve and I intricately planned, we also had many meaningful and insightful discussions. While some of what she told me was disturbing, and even terrifying, I felt closer to her. It seemed that at least some of what she was telling me was actually the truth.

One night, we talked about the disorder, and while I was to find out later that she was still manipulating me like a master, that night I was thrilled that it seemed that she was opening up a bit.

She said things that actually gave me hope, although there were portions that were disturbing. "I do want to get better," she told me but followed with "I feel awful about hurting you and Daddy." I knew it was important that she want to get better for herself. I followed Taryn's lead and journaled some of my own thoughts.

July 2003

Last night we discussed the eating disorder and her feelings about it. . . . She's indifferent on whether she lives or dies . . . and she wants to get better, but it sounds like the main reason is because she feels so bad for Steve and me. She also is baffled and aggravated about why SHE got this disorder. She said she knows she's been raised right, knows she's loved . . . so why is this happening to her?

She described the battle within—how she's sick and tired of feeling weak, and momentarily blacking out when waking, feeling that tremendous hunger and crying from it at night, but also that she's had times of eating normally and has missed the hunger, the high you can get from the hunger.

I told her not to worry about why *she* has this. That this time in her life, for any teen, is full of self-doubt, fears, low self-esteem, problem behavior. It's not about what your problem is, more about what you do about it, how you get past it.

We discussed antidepressants—I think maybe it's worth a shot. I do know she needs to feel better about herself.

The rest of our time in Colorado was like a clock ticking, as we watched Taryn eat less and less. Our car trip home was not unpleasant—we enjoyed our time together, but with each meal, our anxiety grew. There had to be something we could do, and we felt like we had to do something before the damage she was doing became permanent.

CHAPTER SIX

Full Immersion

August to September 2003

The decision to send Taryn to an eating disorder facility was not an easy one. We got back in time for her to go to band camp, an intense two-week "boot camp" of preparation for band members, including the dance line. While we were concerned, neither Nina nor anything I read recommended limiting or withholding her activities. At this point, Taryn was ultrathin, enough so that Steve and I worried about whether she would have the endurance for such a grueling workout in the sweltering Florida summer sun. You didn't have to have a health problem to faint from the exertion; kids did all the time. Somehow, however, she made it through without passing out and, in fact, masked her condition and completed the camp without incident.

This gave me a little boost of hope. Maybe she wasn't so bad—maybe we could get through this by ourselves. The mind is a funny thing. We rationalize and grasp at tiny straws, attempting to talk ourselves into believing the fairy tales we already know, deep inside, aren't really true. I spoke often to Nina, needing the experience she offered, needing someone to tell me if we were safe or in trouble. The problem was, she couldn't really tell us what to do. She could only speak in generalities—she didn't see Taryn responding to their sessions; usually things got worse before they got better; Taryn needed to want to recover.

Our situation was complicated by the issue with the kitchen chef. The police had informed us that Taryn would have to press charges, or they would have to catch him in the act before they could arrest him. We grappled with the idea of Steve going to his home and letting him know, graphically, what he could expect from us if he saw Taryn again. We talked ad nauseam about our limited options and kept as close a watch as possible on our not-so-little girl. The police said they would patrol his house, and we finally had to leave it in their hands.

Back home, I buried myself in research again; this time, looking for inpatient facilities, just in case. I started locally, but within days I had contacted places all over the country. It was hard to accept, but the writing on the wall was getting clearer—there was a good chance we might have to send Taryn somewhere for help, and I wanted to be ready.

Now that Taryn was back in school, the excuses started again—the "I'll eat laters," the "no times," the missed meals.

She was beginning to look unattractively thin. She didn't look like the pictures of anorectics—gaunt, skeletal, or bony. In reality, she looked like a lot of the high school girls, breezing through the halls in their size 0 jeans and tiny tops. When I took her for her annual checkup, she was actually given a clean bill of health. But she didn't look healthy, and it seemed that every day, Taryn disappeared just a little bit more. Steve and I were getting desperate.

I had narrowed down my choices of facilities and called a nationally known treatment center located less than two hours away. As we were going through the process, I was shocked to be told that our insurance would not cover this. It had not occurred to me that, on any planet, this would not be covered like any other disease, disorder, or accident. It had to do with their license, and for us to get any coverage, we would have to send Taryn to a facility with a hospital license.

I spent hours, days, on the phone, trying to make my way now through the insurance maze. And then I was finally down to the handful of places that met the insurance criteria and came highly recommended. Even though they all met the insurance requirement, all of the facilities warned us that there was a risk that our insurer could find a loophole and refuse to pay. In some cases, the risk was almost $100,000. In any case, we would have partial responsibility. When we picked ourselves off the floor, Steve and I knew that, even with insurance, this was going to be a major financial hit. Once again, we questioned, "Are we really at this place? Is she in this much danger?" But, unwilling to put a price tag on our daughter's health, we trudged ahead. We discussed our fears and findings with Taryn, who, while not thrilled with the idea of leaving home for the required two months, did not shut us down with protest.

Then, a highly regarded facility in Arizona called. They had an opening. In less than a week. August 19. Because it was a quick way for them to fill a bed, there would be some adjustment to the price, although we'd still be paying the equivalent of a college education. Panic! Now it was decision time. Put up or shut up. Get help or . . . not.

We agonized over our options. We wished she could be closer, but the place less than three hours away just couldn't guarantee an opening anytime soon. There were just too many kids with eating disorders! Who knew? We preferred the idea of a nurturing setting rather than a hospital setting, and the other two were so far away. "But . . . maybe . . . should . . . would . . ." the questions without answers went on and on.

Decision time had come. We called Taryn into our room and laid out the situation. We described the choices, gave her our opinions, and then handed the ball to her. "This will not work unless you are ready to make the changes," we told her. "This is going to cost a fortune and take our daughter from us for sixty days. We love you so much, we'll do whatever we have to, but this will be a complete waste if you're not willing to do the work and make a commitment to recovery."

When she told us she was, we believed her. And while we still wondered if this was the right thing to do, in the end, we went with our gut instincts. Someone once told me, your gut feeling is the universe telling you what to do, so we quickly made the arrangements, and Taryn and I flew to Arizona.

There were a lot of things I loved about the facility, even before we arrived on their doorstep. Every time I spoke to someone there, they were kind, concerned, informed, and peaceful. I got a good feeling from each individual. I loved their concept of a calming, nurturing ranch, complete with equestrian therapy. I believed in their faith-based approach. And if Taryn couldn't be in Florida, this wasn't a bad second choice. Most of my family lived less than an hour away, which would be handy for visits.

The staff made the transition as painless as they could. It felt a little like she was going to camp. We checked in and then climbed into the van that would take us out to the ranch. I could almost forget that I would be leaving without her. Almost. When we rounded the corner, the horses greeted us, and the neatly manicured western-style buildings stood before us. I blinked back a tear as it hit me—this was Taryn's home for the next two months. We toured the facility with our friendly guide and then headed to the house where she was assigned. The comfortable, homey furnishings made it seem like anything but a hospital, but soon we were at the nurse's station, and it all came rushing back.

We were here to rid Taryn of the evil eating disorder and nurse her mind and body back to health. We saw the large, roomy quarters she would share with three other girls, and I noticed all the stuffed animals and girlish mementos on the beds and bulletin boards. It could have been a college dorm, except some of the residents had tubes in their noses, others were unhappily relegated to the couch, and all of them were carefully monitored by medical personnel.

The nurse at the station on Taryn's floor had angel eyes—the kindest, warmest eyes I'd ever seen. She looked at me with compassion as I finished signing all the papers, and I suddenly realized this was it. It was time for good-bye. And even though the weight of the world had been on my shoulders for the past six months, even though I knew she would have the best of care, my heart broke.

I hugged my daughter, and asking if we could just have a few moments alone, we stepped around the corner. I'll never forget standing in the stairwell, not wanting to let her go, tears running down my face. How had it come to this? How could I walk away and leave her alone in this strange place? Please, dear God, was this the right thing to do?

Too late. It was done. Another facility employee waited to take me to my sister's house in Scottsdale, and her concern and empathy for my sorrow was immeasurable. She reassured me that many a parent had cried in her van. We talked about how attractive so many of the girls were, these girls whose self-esteem had bottomed out to the point of self-destruction. She told me the majority of their patients were high-achievers—homecoming and prom queens, valedictorians, cheerleaders, and dancers.

It was from her that I learned that you could tell what kind of problems a girl had from her personality. She said, "I can tell immediately when I pick them up at the airport. The bulimic girls are bubbly, talkative, lots of personality, and they're not always underweight. The anorectics are quiet, shy, always painfully thin." Where did my daughter fit into this world? I was glad that I'd come with her, and that she hadn't been waiting alone in the airport, waiting to be profiled.

When I reached my sister's house, I was drained. It was hard to believe that when the day began, I'd been home in Florida with my family intact. Although it had only been a few hours, I was desperate to reach out to Taryn, and when my sister's fax machine wouldn't work, we drove to her friend's house.

August 29, 2003

Hi sweetheart. I'm at Aunt Linda's looking out the window and thinking you are looking out over a similar landscape of mountains, deserts, and clouds. Only you are there in a totally new surrounding, with new people, new rooms, and hopefully, the start of a new life. You have not left my thoughts for a moment, and I hope your first night is full of hope and promise—it is definitely full of love, which is being sent across this fax line.

Almost immediately after coming home to Florida, band camp began. I had to attend because of my position on the dance line. It was two weeks of intense physical exercise—all of which was done in the unbearable Florida summer sun. Somehow I made it through on cut-up cucumber for lunch and bits of salad for dinner. All the while my mother kept showing me brochures for inpatient treatments, but I was hesitant to agree to actually go to these lengths.

Finally the time came. Four days into my junior year of high school a facility had an opening and we would get partial coverage from the insurance company. As my parents went over the pros and cons of the situation, I sat wondering what my options would be if I refused to go. Things would get much tenser around the house, and I knew I would only be digging myself into a deeper hole. At least if I agreed to this inpatient thing, then I could have a second chance at my eating disorder. I wasn't going to have to gain too much weight, and I would come out, metabolism fully charged, ready to start my eating disorder again with my parents thinking I was "cured."

So I agreed and was sent for round one in inpatient care. My mom had found a beautiful retreat for women with eating disorders—complete with mental and physical doctors, therapists of all kinds, and horses. Everything seemed perfect about it; it offered every component that figures into the recovery equation, but, unfortunately, I was only there for an intermission.

The first day at the treatment center was fascinating. After all of the admission mumbo jumbo, we were driven out to the complex. It was unbelievable—old Southwestern-style buildings set into the beautiful desert landscape. I could see groups of girls walking to activities, and I stared in awe. This was no hospital by any stretch of the imagination. My mother sat next to me holding back tears, but a small part of me was a little excited.

I remember sitting with her in the stairwell before she left, reassuring me and telling me how I was going to beat this. Tears welled up in her eyes as she hugged me, telling me how much she believed in me and how well she knew I was going to do. I was wondering if I was going to be able to purge.

"Is it your first day?" a shorter girl with black hair approached me slowly as one of the staff ushered my mother out. I nodded and she smiled. "You don't have to eat the grace meal."

"Excuse me, Cassie, is that food talk?" one of the women behind the nurses' station glanced over at us. Cassie shrugged and walked away.

After my mother left, I was taken to a different building where I was given multiple medical tests. I changed into a hospital gown and watched as the nurse checked through the pockets of my T-shirt and jeans. I took careful note of everything as she drew blood, took my blood pressure, and did an EKG. We started to make our way back for orientation when the nurse paused and started talking to another woman with a name tag.

"Taryn, Jennifer is going to take you to eat lunch with the rest of the girls. I'll see you back at the house," and she left with a warm smile. My only thought was of what Cassie had said—and over-whelming fear. Jennifer walked me over to one of the six tables in the main room. There were a few more tables placed on the sides of the room and a big kitchen in the back. There were seven chairs at every table, one at the head and three on each side, the one at the head clearly designated for staff. Girls were scattered around, three to six at each table. Jennifer sat down and explained that usually at meals, I would be required to eat everything on my plate, but today I just would eat as much as I could. The other girls at the table laughed and played games as I stared at my saltines and chicken soup. I sat for the required thirty minutes and managed to finish an applesauce and one pack of crackers.

After going over the countless rules and regulations, I was given my schedule for the week and a giant packet of papers to fill out. I was scheduled to have individual therapy twice a week, family therapy via teleconferences once a week, an appointment with a dietitian once a week, psychiatrist appointments once a week, art, equine, and recre-ational therapy once or twice a week, and medical doctor appoint-ments every two weeks. I would also meet with a psychologist a few times to discuss test results. Everything was extremely regimented and every hour scheduled in. I would go to school and teach myself what I could, worrying that no matter how understanding my AP teachers were, I would never be able to catch up.

Unfortunately my pulse was extremely low and my pulse deficit was much higher than normal, causing blackouts every time I stood up. The nurses put me on "couch rest," which meant I had to sit on the couch most of the time and drink Gatorade or Pedialyte several times a day in the presence of a staff member; I would sip slowly, wondering if it would be possible to pour it into the plastic plant next to me. This also meant I had to sleep next to the nurses' station for the first couple of nights, which in turn meant that I was kept awake by the bright light and the night nurses' voices, and by the time I actually fell asleep, I was woken up seven minutes later at 5:00 AM to have needles stuck in my arm and more Gatorade forced down my throat.

Since I was a new arrival, I was a cause for excitement among the rest of the residents. As I passed my first few days alone on the couch filling out papers, girls would come up to me between activities, asking any question they could get away with: "Who is your therapist?" "What kind of eating disorder did you have?" and "How long have you had it?" Another girl came the day after me, however, and being all of seventy or eighty pounds, she attracted a little more attention. For once I was happy to finally be out of the spotlight. We made small talk as we filled out our information; the questions we really wanted to ask—the ones we knew were impolite and beyond that "against the rules"—were left burning in our psyches.

Her name was Maggie and she was from Tennessee. I was surprised that I actually liked her. I guess I really didn't expect anyone to be anything like me at all. We laughed about how we couldn't put our napkins on our laps and how horrible the "re-feeding diet" of soup and saltines was—and dreamed of the days when we would get medically cleared and be able to flush our own toilets and walk to the cafeteria instead of taking the golf cart. She had never been hospitalized or in rehab before either, so we had a little in common. I later learned that this wasn't uncommon; since we were in an adolescent unit, many of the girls had never been in any kind of facility before.

It was amazing to me how all of these different girls from different backgrounds and parts of the country could all be stuck here with the same illness. Kelly was from the Midwest, beautiful with big blue eyes and blond curls; she was engaged, the valedictorian of her high school, and admitted for anorexia. Hannah was a quiet, very tiny girl from California who had a dark past and a severe, long-running battle with anorexia. Rebecca got up early every morning to shower and fix her hair and makeup—she looked flawless at every event, and it was a mystery to me that someone who looked that perfect could ever have this problem; I found out later her parents had to put locks on the fridge and cabinets because her bulimia was so out of control. Mary was a Northeastern girl in her early teens who seemed happy but was starving to death. And, Christina was a Southern girl with a calm sweetness about her, who later became my closest friend.

And here we all were, clumped into random groups, strangers such a short time ago but now allies and, beyond that, friends. We watched each other suffer through meals together, cried together in group therapy, and lived together in our own little bubble. When girls left, you could tell if they were going to recover or if they would be back where they started in a few short months. Signs of trouble were easy to spot: refusal to eat snacks unless they were required or isolating oneself from the group. And despite the constant admonishments not to, everybody talked.

The thing that baffled me the most was that although we were told to avoid all talk of food and eating disorders, our entire lives were scheduled around food. Depending on your meal plan, there were six designated times blocked out of the day for eating. Every day we had three scheduled snacks, fifteen minutes each, and three scheduled meals, which lasted a half hour each. Snacks were usually an option of three items; if a girl needed to gain weight, she was often required to also have a glass of Boost or a Resource cookie. Meals were one of two sizes, designated by your dietitian, and if you left a single crumb you were at risk for "supplement," which was a glass of Ensure. The nurse would measure out exactly how much you had to drink, and you were given five minutes to finish it or you were restricted somehow. Ensure scared me more than the devil himself, so after having to drink it once, I started eating a little more.

It was difficult living a life that rotated around food, but even more difficult not being able to talk about it like a normal person. I spent hours in therapy of all kinds talking about eating and food, but the minute I sat down to eat, I wasn't allowed to say a word. Even a statement like "the chicken is dry today" was a crime. I met my therapist a few days into my stay and was immediately and pleasantly surprised. His name was Jake and I adored him. He was funny and understanding and seemed to ask all the right questions at the right time. For the first time, I felt like I had someone I could trust and open up to; I let him in—the first person in a long time.

I was diagnosed with EDNOS, or Eating Disorder Not Otherwise Specified. I knew exactly what that meant from reading all the pamphlets: I wasn't thin enough to be anorexic, and I didn't purge enough to be bulimic. I was disappointed in myself; I felt like I had an "almost" eating disorder. Of course, when I came in, I was trying desperately not to be bulimic, so I told them I purged less than I actually did, which might have affected the results. I was desperately afraid of being bulimic—so out of control and gross. I couldn't be bulimic—it was just a stop on the train to anorexia. I didn't want that on my record forever.

In the beginning, I wanted nothing to do with recovery. I lied my little head off about how I was all gung ho about it, but deep down I just wanted out. However, over the course of the first few weeks, I got a glimpse of life without the eating disorder and I actually liked it. I started reading my Bible and paying attention in therapy and trying to want to get better. One day would be good, one would be bad, but overall, I was doing better.

Unfortunately, this didn't last.

CHAPTER SEVEN

A World Apart

August to October 2003

One day, after an eventful afternoon of making beaded bracelets and talking in secret about self-harm and eating disorder websites, I was feeling pretty relaxed. I strolled into my therapist appointment smiling and cheerful. Having told Jake pretty much everything I could think of about myself, I was wondering what was next; I had no idea how unprepared I was.

"I want you to tell your parents about Ben in the next teleconference," and suddenly there wasn't enough air in the room. I just sat there, not knowing exactly how to respond. Ben was the guy I had lost my virginity to—the one who had walked all over me like I was nothing to him. . . . I didn't want to talk about it, and I definitely didn't want to talk about it with my parents. Nevertheless, after an hour-long session, Jake convinced me, and I left with a feeling of horror and dread in the pit of my stomach. It couldn't get much worse than this.

My parents didn't take it very well. There was dead silence for a good minute or so before Jake tried to break the ice. After a few minutes of awkward, difficult conversation, everything around me seemed to collapse, and I went into a full panic attack. Within minutes I was breathing through a paper bag and praying for air. After the session I sat on a corner of the couch and cried for hours until a nurse came over and took me outside to eat—I forced dry chicken down my throat as I thanked her for not making me go to the cafeteria.

A few days later I had another panic attack because of a swollen gland. I was sure it was cancer and I was told the doctor was completely booked for the rest of the day. I cried and cried and of course, when I finally saw the doctor, he told me that it most certainly wasn't cancer, which is exactly what he told me the first time. My anxiety was skyrocketing at an overwhelming rate and I couldn't figure out why. I was put on Seroquel and Zyprexa, tranquilizers to calm my raging, irrational fears. But nothing helped—all I could do was cry. I started to crave my eating disorder and the sanity it seemed to bring me. It was all I could think about.

The next few weeks were hard, waiting for mail and faxes and not seeing all the familiar faces from home. I missed my friends dearly, though surprisingly, the friend to whom I wrote the most never wrote me back. I remember receiving an abundance of letters from my family, Jaime, and even big "We Miss You" cards from my high school, but never one from Kayleigh. I made up scenario after scenario of why she seemed to be MIA, but I never heard a thing for two months.

Everything seemed to be building toward Family Week, which loomed ominously in the future. After the way the discussion about Ben had gone, I was certainly not looking forward to an entire week dedicated to intensive family therapy. I watched my fellow residents at the Mariposa house leave and come back from this event and I could see the wear on their faces. No one came out unscathed.

Back home, the time passed rather quickly. The pain of loss and separation was tremendous—the whole family missed Taryn terribly. On the other hand, there was that sense of relief again. She was in a safe place, getting her physical health back, and getting every opportunity to heal her soul. The monster eating disorder that threatened to take over our lives, the omnipresent sense of doom, was gone. We could once again focus on normal things—homework, sleepovers, family dinners, sunsets at the beach. There was an empty seat at our table, but there was no closed, silent door upstairs.

Taryn was never far from my thoughts. After a few days at home, I wandered into Taryn's room and found a letter she'd left for us.

August 18, 2003

I guess now all I can say is thank you. Well, and I love you, of course. But you know that already. Through all the fighting and the lies I sometimes wonder how you can still love me, and yet you do. You are the greatest examples of love, forgiveness, patience—all of those fun things we struggle with. . . . I know sometimes it seems like I don't appreciate everything you do for me—from birthday parties to family vacations to the little things . . . but I do. I appreciate everything you do for me more than you know, and I only wish I could do a better job of showing it.

Thank you so much for giving me this chance; I will miss you so much. But I'll be home before you know it, and think of you every day in between. I love you so much.

[I wrote this letter out of sympathy. I figured I owed them something for all of the struggles I had caused them, and this seemed like the perfect way to try to get them over to my side again and to stop worrying so much.]

My desire to have all be well again made me forget the lessons I'd learned the hard way. As soon as I read that letter, instead of remembering all of her manipulations, I immediately took it as a positive sign that this step was necessary and would work.

I faxed her at least once a day, sometimes just a quick "here's what's happening," and sometimes a more thoughtful expression. I sent cards, letters, and packages and encouraged her friends and family to write to her. Much to our surprise, for the first couple of weeks, Taryn was on medical restriction, due to low blood pressure, low pulse, high pulse deficit, and other physical problems. She was diagnosed as moderately malnourished. MODERATELY MALNOURISHED! We couldn't believe it— so much for the clean bill of health.

August 23, 2003

Hello my sweet daughter. Well, it's about 4:30 AM, and once again I can't sleep. . . . I'm slightly frustrated by the lack of info I seem to be getting, or not getting, about how things are going for you so far. I think tomorrow I will start reading the book they gave me. I haven't been able to bring myself to do it yet. Just reading the title *First You Cry* made me cry. I spoke with Mrs. Gregory yesterday. She says Amy is having the same problem, and she's very concerned about her. It's scary how many girls are in the same boat, and how many parents don't know. I feel so lucky that we figured out what was happening, and that we were able to get you help; also, that you recognized that you were in need of this extra help. They say that's half the battle.

August 25, 2003

Hi honey. I just said good night to the girls and walked past your room—my heart aches because I miss you so. . . . I started reading the book and there's a great quote, "She cannot recover alone, but she alone can choose recovery." Choose recovery, Taryn—we are all standing with open arms to support you. I love you with all my heart. Momma

She was given a primary therapist, Jake, and we were thrilled when she reported that he was "awesome." Jake seemed to bond with Taryn, and when she would tell us of one "breakthrough" after another, we began thinking that maybe we had done the right thing. I was able to visit her briefly just two weeks after her arrival, and I remember we took a walk around the compound. She was talking about Jake, and that he'd given her an assignment to tell me the truth about something she had lied about in the past.

"I never connected with Nina," she confessed, to my surprise. "I just went and sat there and said what I thought she wanted to hear. I never changed anything, and I didn't really listen to her." Visions of dollar bills flushing down a toilet, along with the memories of our hopes during those months, spun in front of me, but I wanted her honesty.

"Why didn't you just tell me?" I asked, astonished. "I would have found someone else."

"I know," she replied. "I didn't want someone else. I didn't want to get better."

Wow. What to say? All I could think was, *Thank God for Jake.* We got to know him well in our weekly phone therapy sessions, with him and Taryn on one end and various combinations of our family on the other. Mostly it was Steve and I, sitting in our office with our phone on speaker, bent over the desk, listening as secrets were revealed, and through eye contact, communicating our disbelief that this was happening in our family.

This first assignment was a test. At this point Jake had told me that he thought it would help me to tell my parents more about my "experiences." My mother was visiting, so we thought it would be a great time to see how she reacted to something as non-emotionally driven as me not liking my therapist. She was perfect—understanding, ready to listen—everything I could have asked for. However, when it came to confessing about Ben, it was a completely different story.

Dear Mom and Dad—I'm off transport!! I can walk to all
the programs now—how cool is that? I'm not allowed to ride the
horses or do active rec yet though, which stinks, but hopefully that
will change soon. . . . I'm very nervous for our teleconference
tomorrow. I'm scared our relationship will be damaged when you
find out everything about me and about my eating disorder. . . . I
want to apologize for everything ahead of time and to tell you guys
I want *progress*, not an uncomfortable relationship. . . . I get to call
you in an hour, so talk to you then! I miss ya guys a ton, and tell
Taylor and Halli I love them! Luv, Taryn

*It was emotionally difficult to be separated during some
of the more revealing phone sessions, times when I longed
to literally fly through the phone lines and wrap my arms
around my daughter's fragile psyche.* One of these times
was when, with much apprehension and fear, she confessed the
circumstances of the loss of her virginity with Ben. Because Jake
knew we'd read Taryn's journal and knew about Nate, he mis-
takenly thought we knew most of this story as well, and prior to
the session, he encouraged us to just be honest in our response.

As we heard the story, which in Taryn's eyes was a combination of an unwanted sexual advance and her shameful failure to make it stop, Steve and I were shocked and horrified that she'd kept this secret. We felt we'd adequately prepared her for her eventual foray into the world of hormonally supercharged boys. She knew how to make sure a boy knew "no" meant no. In an effort to be truthful, we expressed our feelings honestly, as Jake had instructed us, and our dismay, surprise, and sorrow were apparent on the other end of the phone line. We were truly shocked, so shocked that we couldn't offer her reassurance and comfort. We were quiet and subdued except for the occasional "Oh no." This wasn't the reaction Jake had expected, and as Taryn dissolved in anguish and tears, he ended the session prematurely to tend to his patient. It's hard to describe the distress we felt, sitting in our office chairs helplessly, while 2,500 miles away, someone else was comforting and hugging our daughter.

September 17, 2003

Hi honey! I just had to write tonight because we didn't even have a chance to say good-bye and tell you we love you. Please know that there is nothing you could tell us that would make us not love you, or not forgive you. Today's phone conference had to be so difficult for you, and we both think you are so courageous, and we are so inspired by your honesty. . . . We're sad that this was so intensely painful for you, and we hope it doesn't discourage you from opening up about some of the things you have locked inside that are hurting you.

Above all, we want you to know with absolute clarity that we love you so much that nothing could shake that love from us. That is unconditional. We are totally supportive and want to do everything we can to help you in your recovery. . . . Except for missing you, we are all doing pretty well. We love you so much. Dad and Mom

Except for that disastrous session, most of the sessions were very interesting and thought-provoking. One day Jake asked us what we thought life was all about. He asked me first, and my immediate reaction was to blurt out "Happiness," but then on second thought, I answered, "Love, family." Steve said, "The experiences." Taryn, having been through this, knew what Jake would say. "Happiness is not what life's about," he explained. "There are many times in life when we're not happy, when we experience pain, sorrow, suffering. Life is about love—loving and being loved. And when we learn about love, we have moments of happiness, sadness, and all the other emotions." This was eye-opening for me—the nurturer who always felt the goal was happiness in my family. Jake showed me that letting a child feel sad or miserable is okay; that I didn't have to always "pump them up."

Another day we discussed emotions, our perceptions of which ones were good and bad. We discovered that no emotion was bad, but in fact, all served a purpose. Taryn admitted that she felt shame almost all the time—an emotion that I ranked as one I rarely felt. Taryn revealed that she felt everyone's pain very deeply, and that things that happened to other people affected her in a very personal way. She felt a responsibility, that she should be able to do something to help change their situation. I was starting to believe that we were peeling away the layers around Taryn's core of unhappiness.

This time of reprieve was also a mixed blessing for Taylor and Halli. Their sister was gone, but so was all the tension that they'd been living with since the nightmare began. Taryn's disease was hard for Steve and me to understand and accept, and we could only guess at how it might be imprinting the lives of a fourteen-year-old and a ten-year-old.

September 12, 2003

Hey Taryn . . . I miss you so much. When I got to Mr. St. John's today to tell him I was going to be out the week of the 28th [for Family Week], I started crying because I missed you so much, and he just hugged me and said, "It's going to be okay. She'll be back soon." Taylor

September 12, 2003

I miss u already. I luv u. I will c u in 2 months. I luv u soooo much. I will send u many letters and faxes. Much luv, Halli

Taylor, a freshman in high school, faced all the questions and whispers of Taryn's peers and friends. Taryn, concerned that rumors were potentially more destructive than the truth, asked me to see if the woman in charge of the dance line would talk to the group about her sudden disappearance. The director asked if I would come in and talk to the girls, as she knew disordered eating and extreme dieting was a big problem for many of them, and she saw it as an opportunity to get an important message across. Taryn agreed, and suddenly I found myself in the position of speaking on a subject about which I never dreamed I'd know so much.

September 16, 2003

Hi Taryn! I spoke to the dance and flag line today. You would have been proud of me—no tears, but it wasn't easy! The girls were all great—lots of questions, lots of concern for you, and they all seemed to miss you a lot. I told them about where you were and what kind of difficulties you've had. I tried not to get too specific, but just answer their questions. We talked about the pressures from society and how unrealistic role models are for women, but not men. They were interested in your daily routine . . . what you were and weren't allowed to do. They wondered what made you decide to go, how Dad and I knew there was a problem, and how you were doing physically. Kayleigh made the good point that it's not about the food, it's about something else, and that's how it manifests itself.

I think, as a group, they were extremely interested in the subject, and in you. You have a lot of friends there. I told them that it would not be like you to love the idea of a bunch of people in the auditorium having a talk about you, but that you didn't want to hide this or have people making stuff up, and that you thought it was important to get this subject out in the open. I definitely got the feeling that they were very proud of you. I love you very much; I miss you like crazy, and I'm very proud of you, too! Love, Momma

The truth was, I missed Taryn, but I didn't miss the eating disorder. It was a relief to wake up each morning, do the mental checklist we parents all do as awareness shakes the sleep out of us, and not have that terrible feeling wash over me: "What will happen today with Taryn?" I knew she was safe and in good, loving hands; however, I continued faxing and writing every day, wanting Taryn to know she was still a part of our daily lives, not abandoned. On particularly busy days, I would find myself at midnight making sure I didn't miss a day of telling my girl that I loved her.

Although Taryn and I could only talk during scheduled phone times, I was encouraged to call and get updates from Taryn's nurse station. It's possible they regretted that suggestion. I called a lot. I was dying to know about her physical condition and what was going on in her head. Rather than put this in their competent hands, I wanted to understand exactly what she was going through. Sometimes it almost felt like I was in treatment, because I couldn't really break away from the constant worry. Was this working? Were they figuring her out? Was she accepting the program?

At the facility, the patients progressed through a "level" system, with each level representing a degree of commitment to recovery, from 1 to 4. Each time Taryn moved up a level, my hope was raised as well.

September 20, 2003

Hi babe—it was great to talk with you tonight—you sound really good, and I pray you are feeling as good as you sound. We are so excited about your decision to go for Level 3—we know it means a lot on your part—a lot of hard work, time, and challenges, not to mention the emotional commitment to recovery. You will definitely be in our prayers.

September 24, 2003

In fifty minutes Eastern time, you will be seventeen years old . . . I wanted to be the first to say HAPPY BIRTHDAY!! We are all so excited for you, Miss Level 3!!! And so proud of you, too. It's a huge achievement—wow. I love you SO much! Love, Mom

Missing Taryn's seventeenth birthday was very tough for me. When we were first told about the required Family Week, I had tried to arrange it to coincide with Taryn's birthday, September 25. They were not able to accommodate my request, because Jake was not going to be in town, so this was to be the first time we were not together to celebrate her birthday. I e-mailed friends and relatives, asking them to please remember the big day with a card or letter, so she would know everyone was thinking of her while she was away from home. Everyone responded so generously with gifts and correspondence, and for that I will always be grateful.

Yet even as I missed Taryn, strange sensations of dread and fear about her return began to surface as the days passed. Her homecoming approached, and I remember feeling guilty because my excitement at having her back home was equaled by my apprehension and anxiety over whether she would be "cured."

It was almost an intuition, because most of the news from the ranch was good. I could not seem to shake off this feeling of trepidation, even as her faxes, letters, and phone calls encouraged us to hope for the best.

Dear Mom and Dad . . . Yesterday was such a great day! . . . I actually got up enough nerve to speak up about several issues that were really bothering me. That felt really good. And then I was elected team captain, which was really cool. And of course equine was awesome—we got to walk and trot and go around the barrels. . . . I'm starting to feel better. I'm crying constantly so you'd never know it, but last night I broke down sobbing because I remembered what happiness felt like. My friend said to me last night, "You've changed so much since you've been here—you just seem more comfortable and happier." It makes me wonder if it's the antidepressant. . . . I miss you and love you—keep writing! Luv, Taryn

And then it was time. Five weeks had passed, and we were getting ready to leave for Family Week. We didn't really know quite what to expect, but Steve, Taylor, and I all experienced heightened feelings of anticipation mixed with a few drops of terror. There would be secrets, confessions, lots of therapy. I felt bad about leaving Halli behind, but knew she'd be much happier with our next-door neighbors than sitting in one therapy session after another. Who wouldn't?

And yet, I was looking forward to getting answers.

CHAPTER EIGHT

Family Matters

October 2003

"No way. There is no way I am ready for this. I still have two weeks, right? Can't we wait a little longer? Is this whole thing really necessary anyway? No need to open old wounds is what I always say! I . . . well, honestly, I just wasn't prepared for this. I'm sorry . . . but are you sure we couldn't hold off another week or two?" My hands shook as I held the dreaded "Honesty in Love" worksheet in my unprepared hands. Fear overtook me as I looked at the words dancing across the page, mocking my pain.

Honesty in Love was the term given to an intense family therapy session that took place during Family Week. Basically, Family Week was a week where the parents and sometimes the siblings of the patient visited and went through a tough week of pretty much every type of therapy the center offered. But the Honesty in Love session was by far the worst of all the fun-filled activities throughout the stay.

The worst part about Family Week was that no one talked about it. We would watch the girls before us come and go every day and see the pain etched in their faces. If you were brave enough to ask them the next morning how it was, all they could usually manage was "It's nice to see my family" or "Pretty good, you know." So no one really knew what was coming—only that it seemed to take its toll on everyone.

Luckily, my Family Week group contained one of my favorite girls and my roommate, Maggie, so I knew I would at least have someone to talk to. I had never met the other girl, Rachel, who was in the other house in the adolescent unit. All I knew about her was that she was devastatingly thin when she first arrived. She seemed very quiet and sad.

Family Week is during the sixth week of treatment and by then I had lost my mild interest in recovery. I filled out most of the worksheets honestly though, because very few asked about wanting recovery. Jake knew most of the things my parents did not, so I was afraid he would ask me to tell all my secrets. Fortunately, he seemed to still feel guilty about pressuring me to tell them about Ben, so he didn't try to get me to expose much else.

By the time my parents arrived, my therapist, dietitian, and the rest of the team approved my pass, so I could spend a lot of the weekend outside of the facility with my parents. Everything was going as planned. I was excited to see my family—it had been a long time, and I had forgotten how awkward life had been living at home. I focused on all the faxes and cards and gifts and phone calls from so far away.

Everything started out okay. Family Art Therapy was the first night and everyone seemed emotional, but in a so-happy-we-love-each-other kind of way. And everyone including myself seemed to really like Maggie and Rachel's families, so the week didn't seem like it would be too bad. I tried to seem excited about recovery, everyone cried, and it was interesting seeing all of the projects that were made and what they represented.

Then the fun began. Maggie, Rachel, and I were shuttled every morning after breakfast to the Family Week center for the facility. We met up with girls from the two adult centers and, of course, our families. The first few days were more basic family exercises and simple information. One exercise had everyone in our group imagine a line going across a room where both ends represented extremes. The therapist would make a statement and we would all stand on the line in the area that we felt most represented our emotions. The therapist would say "I really like the way I look," and everyone would scatter, my father the lone man at the "true" end of the line, Maggie, Rachel, and I positioned near the "false" end (all carefully watching the others to see where they placed themselves), and the rest of our family members in between.

Meals were awkward. My mother commented on how unhealthy some of the snacks were, and I slowly stared down the Teddy Grahams I had chosen for my required snack and try to explain how you couldn't call food "bad" or "good." I wondered if she realized how hard those comments made it for me. Couldn't she understand that talking about how the food she was paying people to force me to eat was unhealthy was making me resent this whole charade even more? Didn't she know that I knew far more about how unhealthy all of this damn food was and of course I didn't want to eat it but I HAD TO? It frustrated me and made me angry as I watched her pick at the same food that I would have to later scrape off my plate. I suppose she just didn't know the right thing to do, but sometimes it just seemed so obviously wrong to me.

One morning as we met before therapy, I gave everyone a hug, and my mother exclaimed, "It is so good to hug you now that there is actually something to hug!" She meant well. She didn't realize that in my mind, she had basically called me fat. My father, never at a loss for words in the most important times, came back with "Well, it's always good to hug you!" This brought tears to my eyes and I rushed into his arms. Ironically, even though my father understands my eating disorder the least, he always says the best things.

My mother unfortunately took this the wrong way and even brought it up in therapy later, which made me feel guilty, but proud of my father for what he had said. It made me feel like we had an unbreakable bond—like he knew me so well that he could sense that my mom had made me horribly uncomfortable. And even though I felt bad for rejecting my mother, I couldn't help but love my father more than anything in the world at that moment.

Right up until the Honesty in Love session, I had felt that it was good to see my parents, but I could just sense the elephant that followed us into every room we entered. Flashes of the past year haunted me, and my stomach knotted whenever I thought about it. The days went by quickly until suddenly we were the ones in the center of the room, sharing our secrets.

We went through, one by one, and everything seemed to go well. Nothing too dramatic; we calmly smiled as we listened to each other's lists of amends, offenses, and affirmations. Slowly things started to heat up emotionally.

I watched Taylor meekly tell me about how she tried so hard to keep my secrets but how she was so afraid because I just seemed to be getting sicker. I was flooded with guilt knowing I had put too much pressure on my sweet little sister. But I also remember thinking that she didn't even know half of my eating disorder secrets. I wondered what her breaking point would have been; when she would have told.

I remember looking at my dad and seeing him cry—something I have seen maybe three times my whole life. I remember the knot in my throat because I hated thinking that I had hurt him. Throughout everything, my father never seemed to do anything wrong. He was a quiet bystander who watched with pain in his eyes. I felt like a terrorist killing the innocent; the guilt from hurting someone who in my head had never done anything wrong was too much to bear. I sobbed uncontrollably; I guess my dad never stopped being my hero even after I shot him down.

But that wasn't the showstopper. I stared at my list of offenses toward my mother and wondered if she would finally own up to what had really happened this past summer. I needed to know for my own personal sanity.

"Well, um, my first offense is your dishonesty about your sources of information. It is really hard for me to understand why I have to be completely honest with you about everything, but you don't have to do the same. Like this summer for example: I know that you didn't find out about Nathan the way you did, and I just feel like I should be able to know why," I mumbled nervously. The dead silence that followed reassured me that I was correct in questioning her. She had been lying.

"I read your journal," she said slowly. I searched for remorse in her eyes but found none. I could hardly even hear what she said after that because I was concentrating so hard on my facial expressions. I was brimming so full with pure rage that I had to keep control over how I looked to everyone else. I couldn't say anything for a while. I had to compose myself, put together a thought. I stared at her, thinking about what I could say that would make everything okay again.

I managed something about her being brave and I appreciated her risking ruining our relationship to save me. I felt like I was on a stage. I cried and put on a show for everyone around me—telling a story of forgiveness and happy endings. But inside I was seething. I clenched my jaw with pure anger and ferocious rage, which brewed in my soul. She couldn't do this to me. Right then I wanted to go home and drop fifty pounds. I would show her that reading that journal had ruined our relationship and hadn't even fixed anything. She would pay.

I smiled through the pats on the back and praise from everyone around me. I was the good daughter who forgave and moved on; everything would be okay now. The other mothers told me how much they thought of me for forgiving her, and Maggie commended me for my courage. Everything was a blur. All I could see was red. The week ended quickly and I said good-bye to my family with much apprehension. I knew it wasn't over. Two more weeks and I would be home again, and if all went according to plan, back into the eating disorder in less than three. I wasn't sure at all how I felt—there were too many emotions: anxiousness, excitement, happiness, fear, and even a little sadness at leaving. After all, I had made some great friends and would miss the now-familiar settings. I couldn't sleep well that night thinking about everything. So much emotion, so little time.

Taylor, Steve, and I walked down the Phoenix, Arizona, Jetway. We weren't sure what was in store for us, but we all felt both excited and nervous. I quickly called our next-door neighbors to make sure Halli had gotten over her initial teary reaction to her family leaving without her, and sure enough, she had. Our wonderful friends had immediately made her feel secure and right at home. I wondered if the rest of the week would be so easy.

My parents lived within thirty minutes of the center, so we stayed with them during our Family Week visit. We were glad we had made those arrangements, as it gave us a chance to decompress each night after a full day of exhausting mental and emotional dissection.

I really didn't know what to expect from Family Week. I knew that most of these facilities had family programs and requested that at least parents participate. At our center it was required, and it was no streamlined affair—we had six days of "communication enhancement, family dynamics, education, and group therapy sessions" ahead of us. This told me that many, if not most, of the patients had family issues involved in their disorder. I didn't have a clue what ours would be, but I was interested to find out, especially if it meant Taryn would stop trying to self-destruct.

Our first morning of Family Week started early. We were anxious to get started. Although none of us had spent a lot of time in therapy, and there was still a small voice in the back of my head shouting, "what the heck are we doing in this room," I wanted to get some answers. I trusted that this place would know how to do that. We were thrilled when Taryn walked in with the other girls, and happy to see how well she looked.

Our first day was a bit of an orientation, where we learned some basics about eating disorders and what our schedule would be like. It became clear that the "main event" was a highly anticipated session called "Honesty in Love." The patients had been preparing for this session almost from the time they arrived. That first day, we were given information and worksheets that would help us get ready for the two Honesty in Love days. We were all divided into groups, and we were introduced and given time to get to know the two families with whom we would be sharing our Family Week.

Our family appreciated the opportunity to talk to other parents and siblings who were going through similar experiences. Although the idea of eventually sharing deeply personal information in front of virtual strangers was unsettling, I didn't feel like we had an awful lot to hide. Still, we had to get used to the idea that these would be basically open sessions. We soon felt a close bond with these moms, dads, brothers, and sisters who clearly cared about their daughter or sister, just like we cared about Taryn.

Everything was perfectly planned, from the residents' arrival at the separate Family Week facility, to the communication games we played, to the songs sung during the chapel time. We learned about how our daughters' nutritional plans were developed and heard stories of desperation and hope. We were taught the way to say something without shutting down the lines of communication, or hurting someone's feelings, by following a three-step plan, a basic tool of therapy.

First, you made a "When you . . ." statement, then an "I feel . . ." statement followed by an "I need or would like . . ." declaration. For example, "When you tell me a lie, I feel betrayed and sad. I need you to try harder to be honest." We thought this made a lot of sense, and all of us became very aware of how we were communicating. Soon, we even joked around with it, creating little paragraphs of nonsense.

We especially enjoyed our session of art therapy, where we saw some of the projects Taryn had created to express her innermost thoughts. We were also asked to do our own project to illustrate how the eating disorder had impacted us, or how it looked to us. Mine was an enormous black boot stomping down on our family, and Taryn's was even more interesting. She'd formed a clay figure of herself and made a black curtain around it, open on top, representing the eating disorder. She said the curtain could move, but it was something she could hide behind. God, however, could see her real self from above. I was amazed at her use of symbolism.

One thing that struck us as strange was the snack food that was provided for breaks. There were Oreos, all kinds of chips, and other junk food. It seemed counterproductive to me to encourage the girls to eat unhealthy food, but the reasoning behind it, as Taryn explained, was that there was no "good" or "bad" food. Food was food, and the residents had to relearn how to eat again. I wasn't sure I agreed with this, but then, I wasn't the expert.

The Honesty in Love worksheet basically provided an outline for us to organize our thoughts in preparation for the intense familial exchange that was to help us restore trust and resolve anger and frustration. Taryn's preparation involved disclosing the things she'd learned about herself as to why the disorder developed and to admit to the behaviors and events that had contributed to it.

Part one of our worksheet asked how the eating disorder or other addictions impacted our lives. I answered, "When you engaged in eating disordered behavior, I felt profound fear, times of helplessness, sadness, and guilt, and I've wondered if I could have somehow seen or done something to help or prevent it. I've spent hours, days, and weeks researching, finding the right place, learning, talking, getting your team. Your eating disorder is now a part of my life. It's taken an emotional toll, a financial toll, a physical and mental toll. It's created great stress. It's also opened a new world to us, provided a challenge for us to overcome, and perhaps, hopefully, been a gateway to better family communication."

What a relief to finally say that out loud! I didn't think Taryn had given one thought to how we, her family, had been affected by her issues, and I welcomed the opportunity to actually communicate that to her. I felt like this was one of the most important aspects of Family Week. We were getting the chance to finally learn how we had gotten to this place, but she was also learning how we felt about it.

The second and third part of Honesty in Love was "Amends and Offenses"—asking for forgiveness for things you felt you did to hurt your loved one and describing the ways your loved one hurt you. Finally, we ended with "Affirmations," where we described Taryn's character traits that we enjoyed, admired, and respected, and then shared favorite memories.

I wrote down, "Your marvelous sense of humor, your compassion and need to give, how deep a thinker you are, your ability to be independent and organize and accomplish what needs to be done. I love your gentle spirit, and I admire who you are. I admire your ability to express yourself through words—what a magnificent writer you are."

I continued, "I have countless memories: scratching your back, making sand castles, watching you dance and smile, skiing and snorkeling with you."

As prepared as we all thought we were, we were not ready for the emotional sledgehammer called Honesty in Love. Our group, made up of three families, was together in a large room. Each family would take its turn, with the other families sitting in a circle around them, listening and absorbing the unfolding drama. And it truly was a drama.

Although I came away feeling our family was basically very healthy, it was devastating to learn the depths of Taryn's lack of self-esteem. Good grief, what else could we have done to try to help her develop a positive self-image? We had heaped praise and encouragement on her continually as she grew up, verbally rewarding her for each accomplishment, large and small. To learn that as far back as kindergarten she'd belittled herself was a blow to our own parental self-esteem. To hear about middle school quite simply broke my heart.

Of course, I knew almost all the stories she told. She had told me a lot of her insecurities, often at bedtime. We would talk, sometimes for a long time, as I'd try to reassure her and give her advice. Later she would tell me how things had turned out, and I was always under the impression that we had worked through the problem. Now I was hearing that nothing had really been "worked through" in Taryn's mind, and since I was her mother, and had to love her, my assurances pretty much meant nothing.

Taryn's low self-esteem, combined with her perfectionism, sensitivity, and chemical imbalances, which produced depression and anxiety, made her a perfect candidate for this particular disorder. Couple that with the pressure to be thin from her peers, the dance line, and society in general, and the cause of her eating disorder started to make sense. While one girl might experience many of the same things and cope just fine, another will find herself losing her grip on her distorted reality. And while Taryn fell hard, seeing and hearing the stories of some of the other residents made us realize how devastating this disorder could be.

During Honesty in Love there were many tears, and they weren't limited to the family in the middle of the circle. The two therapists who facilitated the sessions were skilled at getting everyone to open up and speak directly to the issues. As we sat on the outside, listening to the others process their pain, we were drawn into the familiar stories and reactions. And while many things didn't apply to us, there were common areas, especially the pain and frustration all the parents felt while trying to cope with their daughters' illnesses.

Two things stood out for me from our session. One came during Taylor's moment of Honesty in Love. She was in the spot-light, speaking directly with Taryn, guided by her trusty worksheet. One part of her fourteen-year-old self wanted to gig-gle through some of this, making light of the whole situation. Another part, a deeper part of her consciousness, felt more than any of us had guessed.

As my sweet-natured middle child began talking about how the eating disorder had affected her, emotions started playing out across her face. "You told me what you were doing, and then I had to keep your secrets," she said quietly. "And then I became afraid that you would die, and it would be my fault because I didn't tell anyone," she confessed, sobbing, the tears spilling from her eyes.

The responsibility that she had felt over the past months became apparent to everyone in the room. Quiet, muffled sniffles could be heard, as empathy filled the space. I didn't care that it wasn't time for a break—the mother-guilt overwhelmed me and I held her as tight and as long as I could. How had I not known that she struggled with this duty, this vow to silence that threatened every fiber of her being? Shouldn't I have seen that she was fighting a no-win battle within—that loving her sister meant choosing between keeping her secret or saving her life?

But we weren't through yet. It was my turn, and so far, there hadn't been any major surprises. Of course, the saying goes, "Save the drama for your mama," and there was no exception in Honesty in Love. We went through the first part about how the disorder affected me. On to Amends, breezed through Offenses, and there we were, heading for the finish line, when Taryn said, "Oh, one more thing. . . ." All eyes in the room turned to her, as she quizzically asked, "I'm just wondering—this summer, when you found out about Nathan and how bad my eating disorder was . . . how DID you find out?"

My moment of truth. Or should it be? How should I answer? There was silence in the room, and like a tennis match, all eyes swiveled from Taryn . . . to me. If I told her about reading the journal, how would she react? Would she scream at me in anger?

Would we destroy all this trust we'd built up during Family Week? Why wasn't she asking Steve this question? He read the journal, too. But I was the bad guy again, taking the heat.

In the end, I just couldn't lie to a direct question, eye to eye.

"I read your journal," I responded, quietly, but very firmly. "I chose between respecting your privacy and saving your life. I knew something was very, very wrong, and we weren't getting the truth from you, and I was desperate to know how to help you." As she sat staring at me, I began to cry, and I said, "I would have done anything I had to do—I was so scared."

Moments passed—it seemed like hours. And then Taryn responded in a way I never expected. She didn't yell, her face didn't harden in anger, she didn't turn away. The tears running down her face matched mine as she said with a small smile, "I'm glad I have a mom who cares enough about me to risk losing my trust so she could help me." I dissolved in emotion. It was difficult to finish my session, but I deeply wanted to do the Affirmations and let her know how much I admired, respected, and loved her.

Later, both the moms in our group came up to me. They hugged me and said, "I would have done the same thing." And while I'll never feel good about breaching that trust, at that moment, I knew I would do it again in a heartbeat if I had to.

Since Taryn had achieved Level 3 status, we were able to cap off Family Week by taking her out to dinner with the other families in our group. The next day, we all went to my sister's house for a party. It was the first time that Taryn shared meals without supervision since coming to the center, and we were all a little nervous about it. We were instructed what to watch for and how to react in different situations.

Without making it obvious, everyone was aware of what Taryn ordered, how much she ate, even how she ateT. Everyone tried to act like everything was normal, but there was a lot of walking on eggshells. It felt very much like trying to gradually reintroduce a castaway or a prisoner of war back to the traditions of society.

I was happy to have Taryn back in the family fold, and there were many hopeful signs that weekend. Jake thought she was ready, her nutritionist thought she was ready, and Taryn indicated that she really wanted recovery. The occasional awkward moments, however, were reminders that in two weeks, she would be home. Home, without Jake, where no one would be monitoring her meals, watching her daily vital signs, or accompanying her to the restroom. Not even me. Especially not me.

I could feel the first rumblings of panic in my stomach.

CHAPTER NINE

True Lies

October to December 2003

October 14, 2003

   Mom and Dad—I miss you guys already and you only left yesterday. I can't wait—I hope this is the fastest two weeks *ever*. I can't
wait to get back to my life. I'm sending you a list of my binge foods
and snack foods, so you can have the "dos & don'ts" as you called
it. Some of the binge foods you might not be able to get rid of, but
I'll have to get used to having trigger foods around anyway . . . I
love you!!

As Taryn counted down the hours to her departure from the ranch, I found myself in a completely contrary state of mind. One minute I would smile as thoughts of her home-coming would flash through my mind. I would read her anxious, hopeful words and pray that her arrival would mean our family's full circle back to the way it was before the nightmare began eight months earlier. But the next minute, while those thoughts were still lingering, my mind's pendulum would swing in the opposite direction. I was so unsure about my role in Taryn's return to the real world. The fear of having her struggle with recovery on my watch, back in my home, was sometimes over-whelming. I didn't feel confident in my ability to just "let go," and I didn't know how I could take it if she relapsed. So much hope hung in the balance. Our family's base of stability and hap-piness was riding on this. What if she wasn't better?

And then I'd think of something she'd said during Family Week, or my latest conversation with Jake, who was so positive about Taryn. And I'd miss her and think about how much I wanted this to work. Back and forth, back and forth—these involuntary what-ifs played out in my brain. But as the days clicked off the calendar, it seemed each night I went to sleep with an unexplained, nagging feeling of dread.

The bottom line was that she was safe at the center. While she was there, I could rest easy that someone was looking after her. Someone was making sure she ate right, that her activities were healthy and therapeutic, and that she received the right medicines and got enough sleep. Someone was monitoring her weight, her moods, her health—mentally, physically, and spiritually. At home, there were too many uncertainties. Too many potential traps. Too much freedom and too many things that could go wrong. And suddenly, it was time.

October 17, 2003

Hi darling—I know this is probably going to be a pretty rough day. I bet you've already been through the worst of it though, with your good-byes to Jake. These people have been there with you through some tremendous turning points, and I know Jake, especially, has become such a trusted confidant. I hope that you will find the same compassion, understanding, and wisdom in your team here that you found there. Just know you have *all* of our love and support, and we are hardly able to contain our excitement at having you home again. TWO DAYS!!

My last weeks at the treatment center were filled with daydreams and excitement. At this point, I had absolutely no intention of recovering, so it was just a patient wait until I was discharged and back on my own. The girls who I had grown so close to were all leaving since their two months were up, so I watched the new girls and tried to pick up on their tricks. The new girls were still naive enough to think they could get out of rehab easily without manipulation, so they bragged about how they had achieved such startlingly low weights. I carefully took mental notes.

Memories of the day I was discharged come to me in a hazy blur. I remember a patient coming barreling down the stairs screaming "GIVE ME MY FUCKING BOOKS BACK!!" and I smiled as the nurse handed me my sack lunch. I vomited it up on the plane a few hours later. I raced around in the Atlanta airport on my layover, stocking up on binge food and purging twice more on the second plane home. And at the end of the day I stood in my kitchen, drinking a glass of cran-grape juice to prove to my parents that I was totally back to normal. I gagged as I forced down the sugary fluid; I smiled to make them feel safe.

The first few days I tried to take it slow. I figured if I suddenly stopped eating, my metabolism would crash and I would lose the advantage I had gained from eating normally for two months. My nutritionist and I had every meal planned out to the carrot stick, and I started the first day by cutting the calories of my afternoon snack in half. A few days later I cut it out altogether. My mother was told that staying on my meal plan had to be my responsibility, so she tried to back off as much as possible; besides, I was back to school full-time, so the only meal she could monitor was dinner.

It was pretty much downhill from there. I fell hard and fast, and this time I really knew what I was doing. I stopped eating lunch next, then breakfast, and because of late dance rehearsals and other excuses, I finally managed to even escape from dinner several nights a week. By the time I had been home a month, I was hardly eating more than an apple a day, and if I did, I threw it up in plastic bags in my bedroom. My closet began to stink because I could only take out the puke-filled bags a couple times a week; my parents rarely left me home alone. I went back to dance line and ballet, and I remember gaping at my body in the mirror during class. I realized that I was, without a doubt, enormous.

By the time I arrived back in Florida, my mother already had a lot of my "recovery team" in place. During my last few sessions with Jake, I had interviewed a few therapists, listening for the one that I could bear talking to for more than five minutes. As soon as I got home, I already had an appointment with the top two therapists.

The first woman struck me as very Freudian and weird. She was older and kept talking about my childhood and "digging up things from the past." Frankly, she seemed like a lot of work, which I had absolutely no interest in. The second, Kit, I almost immediately liked. She was much younger, and she really seemed to listen to what I was saying. The things she said actually seemed to apply to my life, and I enjoyed talking to her. Even though I wasn't planning to take any of her advice, she seemed like a person that I could spend an hour with.

The nutritionist my mother had gotten, Nancy, was supposedly the best in our area. She was very up front and didn't seem to trust me. I lied to her all the same, but she figured it out pretty quickly. She quit within a few months and told me to call her when I was serious; she said it wasn't fair to waste her time and my parents' money. It seemed to me like one less person to worry about.

I returned to high school two months into my junior year. Instead of letting rumors of pregnancy and jail time surface while I was gone, my mother had spoken to the girls with whom I danced. Everyone knew exactly where I had been and how long I had been there, so it was awkward at best. People who never really acknowledged me were acting like we were best friends. Some people who I thought were my best friends were suddenly distant. Nobody asked any questions until I had been back for a few months, and even then the questions were vague and nervous. I worked hard to catch up on the dance line, learning a new routine so I could perform in the last couple of football games.

At my high school, there were two separate dance teams. Dance line, which I had been on for three years, performed at the football games with the marching band. Dance team was an off-season competition team that was much more difficult to get on; however, I decided to try out this year because I had missed most of the dance line season. My coach, who had been nothing but supportive of this whole crisis, both suggested and encouraged the idea.

Imagine my rage when I didn't make the team. I knew I should have. If I wasn't a better dancer, then I certainly had some seniority over some of the other girls, and I knew I should have been put on that team, especially since trying out was at the suggestion of my coach. It turned out I didn't make it because of my bulimia. My coach had decided after try-outs that I was "too weak" to keep up with the rest of the girls. The irony is that eight out of the ten girls who tried out for the team were obscenely thin and had eating disorders; they just weren't open about it. That was my last straw. I hated myself for not making the team, and I hated my coach for using me as an example. I was one of the only girls who admitted to having a problem and now I was being penalized for it. I could hardly contain my fury.

I started bingeing all the time, at least six or seven times a day. Sometimes I purged, sometimes not; honestly, I felt so depressed and disappointed in myself that I didn't really even care anymore. I gained a significant amount of weight as a result and settled at around 140 pounds. I refused to get on the scale because I was ashamed and couldn't bear to look at the number. At 5'8" tall, 140 pounds is not even close to overweight, but to me, it was insanely huge.

After school I spent hours wandering through grocery stores. I would slowly walk down each aisle, carefully selecting any item that looked good. I would spend up to $100 a day of money saved from my previous jobs on this food, eating it afterward in my car and then throwing up in the store next door. People would stare as they drove by at the girl sitting in her car with chocolate smeared across her face stuffing entire quarts of ice cream down her throat. As I walked up to the store where I would purge, I would look in the windows at my gaping belly and pretend I was pregnant. I liked to look in the mirrors on my way out, too; this time, though, I was a skinny model, not a pregnant teen.

About a month after being home I got a job as a bar-girl at a 1950s-style burger joint. My job was easy, consisting of taking to-go orders and making milkshakes for the servers, and I loved it. It was such a complete reversal from my previous job as a high society host-ess, and I eagerly traded my heels for a pair of khakis and a cook's apron, which I tied around my waist. Plus, I had access to all the milkshakes I could drink, which is every bulimic's dream come true.

A billion milkshakes, plus fries and onion rings taken from the kitchen, and a meal at the end of every shift created a scenario that had me purging at least twice a day at the restaurant. During the win-ter, which is South Florida's busy season, I would get behind in my work because I was sneaking too many purge breaks. A few of the waitresses heard me and everyone started to look at me differently. Most of the people that worked there had various issues of their own, ranging from eating disorders to drug problems. Once the word got out that I was bulimic, the staff suddenly began to treat me as a friend instead of an upper-middle-class, white high school student. I still had to hide the bulimia from the managers, but I loved this world where most people knew my secret and didn't care. Work was fun and I was good at my job—it was my one safe haven where I didn't have to hide my bulimia and I felt completely free and comfortable.

By the end of the semester, I had gained five more pounds. I hated myself but was completely out of control. I had a calculus teacher who said to me, trying to be sweet and helpful, "Oh look, you have gained more weight! You look great!" My jaw dropped. I couldn't believe what I had just heard. As I walked out the door, still in total shock—a friend saying supportive things and trying to make me feel better—I swore to myself I would lose weight. And fast. I swore that I would never get this fat again. And I managed to lose thirty pounds within the next three and a half months.

She was home. Finally home. And I wanted to do everything right. There was no more denial of the magnitude of the problem. There were no more false hopes that this would resolve itself or just disappear. Her time at the ranch had convinced us that somehow, some way, our daughter had fallen down a dark hole. And only she could climb her way out of that hole. Our role in her recovery was going to be very small.

I wanted to do my part, although a good portion of the time I wasn't quite sure what that meant. I didn't want to have any foods hanging around that might trigger her bulimia. I wanted everything to be as normal and relaxed as possible so she wouldn't feel that all eyes were on her. I clung to the hope that maybe she could just slide back into her life without a big adjustment period. And I wasn't the only one.

The rest of the family was excited about having Taryn back in our midst as well. I think the girls, while seeming to take everything in stride, were ready to have their sister back—the sister who was fun, lovable, and made them laugh, not the one who shut herself in her room, made the upstairs smell like rotten perfume, or took her frustrations out on them. Steve was looking forward to getting things back to the way they were supposed to be. He wanted the daughter back who he understood. And he thought that was her getting off the airplane.

I worked hard to have Taryn's "team" in place, so there would be only a minimal interruption in her therapy, as she transitioned from being an inpatient to an outpatient. I made countless phone calls, then researched and interviewed almost twenty different therapists and almost a dozen of our area's leading psychiatrists and nutritionists.

I asked endless questions. We had been given a guideline and I followed it faithfully. "Do you have experience with adolescents?" "What are your professional credentials?" "What is your training in eating disorders?" "What type of therapy do you use?" "Do you stress communication with other professionals your clients see?" Costs, insurance, appointment protocol—I began to get pretty good at weeding through and discovering the person behind the diploma.

We had been encouraged to have a four-pronged line of defense waiting at home. The most important link would be the primary therapist, with whom Taryn would spend at least two hours a week. She would have monthly visits with a psychiatrist, who would monitor her meds, and weekly visits with a nutritionist to develop meal plans, observe Taryn's weight and nutritional status, answer questions, and generally try to help keep her on the path. They also suggested one or two sessions a week with an adolescent eating disorder support group, to continue the practice of group therapy.

I knew whoever we chose for the therapist had big shoes to fill. I was concerned because I knew Taryn had honestly let down her guard with Jake. She'd allowed him to get inside her mind, and she'd formed an attachment. The ranch had a strict rule—once the patient left, neither she nor her parents could speak to her therapist again. She could write to him, but he could not write back. She could talk to an aftercare counselor, but not to that primary therapist. Ever. Again. The finality of that would be hard on Taryn, I knew, but I hoped against hope that Jake's replacement would somehow find a way to reach her like he did.

I was like a madwoman, searching for just the right person to take Jake's place. It was so important to find someone who could just take up where he left off, someone Taryn would confide in and trust. I hadn't learned my lesson yet. I still felt like if I just did everything right, things would be okay. We had just given up a pile of money and two months of our dwindling time left with our daughter, and I was determined it wouldn't all be for nothing. I wasn't taking any chances that we could end up back in that parental hell we'd been in.

In my eyes, the first week seemed to go pretty well. It was a flurry of activity, trying to get Taryn's "team" finalized and her schedule organized. While still at the facility, Taryn and Jake spoke on the phone with several therapists, and together, narrowed the group to three. During the first week home, she met with the finalists and decided on Kit.

Kit was my first choice, so I was relieved. She had a background in eating disorders and came highly recommended. Kit was earthy, real, calm, patient, a great listener, and not judgmental. She was a nurse-practitioner in psychiatry, so she would be able to wear two hats as Taryn's psychiatric provider and therapist. It simplified the process, which I thought was a good thing. Life at this point was complicated enough for all of us.

Taryn was also satisfied with the woman I had chosen to be her nutritionist, Nancy. She was no-nonsense, an easy conversationalist, and fun. Taryn seemed to like her, and they immediately got into meal-planning and strategies. From the outside looking in, Taryn's recovery was right on track.

The only piece of the recovery puzzle that appeared to be missing was the support group. It just did not exist in our area. There were adult support groups, but the ranch warned us about those, saying the younger girls often learned the wrong things from the older women. Knowing how prevalent eating disorders were becoming in our community and in society in general, I was concerned that there wasn't even one adolescent support group to be found. I decided to make that my mission.

But before I began throwing myself into that job, I set up a meeting between Taryn and the daughter of an acquaintance. Betsy was about six years older than Taryn, out of college and in recovery from a devastating bout with anorexia and bulimia. She was a gorgeous, athletic girl, engaged to be married, and full of enthusiasm and energy. I felt that, given the void of support groups, it could only be helpful for Taryn to talk to someone close to her age who had walked the walk and had a successful recovery.

I was also determined that Taryn should reenter the high school scene with as little fuss as possible. Before she even came home, we discussed her plans for school, dance line, and so on, and we decided to plan a pre–football game dinner for the dance line, so Taryn could get back into the social swing of things.

It was wonderful to have the house full of girls who were happy that Taryn was home. It was a fun afternoon, and I remember thinking how normal it all was—all the laughter, and girls chowing down on baked ziti, salad, and all the trimmings, including a giant cookie cake. No "cake challenges," portion issues, or eating one lettuce leaf at a time. It was normal. Finally.

Unfortunately, as time passed, so did my feelings of relief and happiness. In their place came uneasiness and a gut feeling of dread. We had our family back, but my intuition was kicking into high gear. Steve, Taylor, Halli, and I wanted so badly for things to be all better, and the others seemed to let their high hopes blind them to the little signs and quirks in Taryn's behavior. I knew, though: something just wasn't right.

She was faithfully attending all her therapy sessions, but I knew that was no guarantee of anything. After all, she herself told me how she sat through all those early therapy appointments with no intention of changing anything. Was she doing that again? I couldn't shake the suspicions or my general sense of foreboding and apprehension. I spoke to Kit and Nancy about my fears, and both also felt Taryn's problems were far from over. Our alliance to help her was firmly in place, but it was still up to her to actually stick to her recovery plan.

She was attending classes and after-school activities, yet she didn't seem to be making much of an effort to get her social life started again. She also didn't appear to have her usual energetic drive. She was sleeping too much and didn't seem to care about school, which was unusual for her. She even became apathetic about taking the SAT test. She didn't really prepare, didn't get a good night's sleep, and overslept, almost missing the test. This was just not characteristic of Taryn.

Her weight, which was often a barometer of how she was doing, was hard to read. She looked healthy and seemed at a good weight, but I was now smart enough to know that this told us nothing about possible bulimic behavior. Her big sweatshirts hid what was underneath. I had to depend on her two specialists to keep track of her weight, as I wasn't supposed to even ask her about it. And as the weeks went by, she began to balk at following her meal plans and was evasive with Nancy.

The nutritionist voiced her concerns to me, reinforcing the mantra that Taryn needed to want this; I could not fix this for her. Eventually she told me she needed to stop wasting our time and money, and I begged her, panic-stricken, "Please stay, please don't quit." She knew I felt helpless and terrified, hearing from a professional that my daughter was not following the program, but she was immovable. "There's no point until Taryn is begging me to come back," she gently assured me.

My fears built up until I found myself back in a familiar dilemma, talking to Steve. "I know things are bad. I know she's back in trouble," I told him, not knowing she hadn't stopped being in trouble. "I have to find out what's going on and what we're dealing with."

Steve agreed. It was time to go on the offensive again. It wasn't as hard this time. I knew Taryn's life was at stake, and I needed knowledge if I was to help at all. But somehow, I had forgotten the kick in the stomach I'd felt when I first read her journal months earlier. I'd forgotten the wave of betrayal I'd felt when I discovered that her real world was a stark contrast from the world she chose to share with us.

Finding the journal was easy. Once again, reading it was horribly difficult. "Never stopped" . . . "puking on the plane" . . . "eating one apple today" . . . "I'm so huge." Oh my God! No, no, no. It just couldn't be this bad. She sounded even worse than before, counting minute calories and listing her purges. I sat on the floor of her bedroom and cried, in complete agony.

Now what? First I called Steve. Then I called the aftercare specialist at the ranch. Next was Kit. "What do I do? What do I say?" And the answer was . . . nothing. It was up to Kit to work with Taryn and get her to admit this. Kit had to help Taryn arrive at a place where she truly wanted to recover. Steve and I needed to back off and leave it alone. We needed to basically ignore the behaviors. We could ask her how she was doing; we could ask if she needed help—the advice went completely against the grain of our parental instincts.

It's hard to describe the helplessness you feel when you realize your child is in serious trouble and your mission is to do nothing. When your natural impulse screams intervention, and the experts you're paying tell you to take a backseat, it's almost too hard to bear. I began to feel like my legs were cut off as a parent. I couldn't react or discipline as I wanted to because it could impact her negatively during this sensitive time.

One example was when the mother of one of Taryn's friends called with some information she'd overheard. That night I sat down with Taryn to discuss it. The following journal entry was written after our very brief conversation:

I am very angry and frustrated. . . . Tonight I told Taryn I found out about her smoking pot in Colorado with the Jamaican stranger. I told her how dangerous this was and so on, and she said, "I made a mistake; I haven't done it since, and I don't want to talk about it. I'm going to bed."

I feel like I'm trapped. I can't say what I feel because I'm afraid to criticize for fear it could "harm her fragile ego." But I can't just let her do and say what she wants. I feel like I can't parent because I could damage her.

I want to tell her to snap out of it. I'm frustrated because we've tried so hard, given up a lot, and given so much, always trying to say, do, and react the right way, and she's still going to screw up her life. She's determined to do things she knows are wrong and dangerous. Steve said tonight he's starting to feel like she won't achieve her potential.

Here was a girl who had all the potential in the world and seemed hell-bent on throwing it all away. But I kept thinking she would pull out of this. When Steve voiced his fear that Taryn might not reach her dreams, it was the first time I honestly realized her actions could devastate more than her physical health. It could actually destroy her future.

It had already affected her participation on the dance line. She didn't express much desire to actually perform in the last couple of football games, although she dressed and was part of the group. And although the director encouraged Taryn to try out for the winter season's dance team, she later called me into her office to tell me she'd changed her mind. Although she admitted that Taryn was one of the better dancers, she expressed a concern that she might not have regained enough strength for some of the more strenuous dance moves. She didn't want to risk an injury with an already fragile girl.

Of course, by the time she'd called me in to give me the news, it was a done deal. The list had been posted. The damage was done. I didn't even know Taryn had tried out. I would have discouraged her, because the ranch recommended avoiding competitive situations for at least six months. I knew in my heart that the emotional benefits of being part of the team far outweighed the downside of possible injury. But it was too late.

I talked to Taryn about what the director had told me. She was angry that she was not included because of what "might" happen, and that it wasn't based on the quality of her dancing. I thought her anger was actually a good thing—at least she wasn't repressing her feelings. But she found a way to bottle up her emotions anyway. After expressing her fury about the decision, Taryn soon began pulling away from all but a few friends. She simply put the dance line behind her and closed the door.

Throughout this time, I continued to reach out to her. I would still go up to tuck in my girls, and I'd always spend a little extra time scratching Taryn's back and chatting, trying to draw out the troubled soul inside. She would tell me just enough to make me feel like I was making a little progress, on a good day. Or she'd confide something that would leave me wondering just how deep and desolate was this prison in which my daughter had locked herself. She could so easily push my buttons, so easily manipulate my emotions. My love for her made me an easy mark, because I felt helpless and I just wanted her to be well.

It was during one of those back-scratching sessions that I first noticed the small, red, slightly scabbed-over slashes on her arms. My world suddenly went from bad to worse.

CHAPTER TEN

The Belly of the Beast

December 2003 to March 2004

I knew Taryn had toyed with the strange and frightening behavior of cutting. I remembered her telling me the previous August that she had cut herself shaving on her ankle, and then noticing a few days later, when she forgot to replace the Band-Aid, that the cut was a carefully constructed X shape, certainly not the usual shaving nick.

And during some administrative part of getting Taryn into the facility, I remembered self-harm was listed as one of her issues, based on information she'd given them. That had made me silently question the occasional cut or scratch I had seen, for which Taryn always had a reasonable explanation. Jake had asked if I was aware that she had indulged in self-harm, and we had discussed it because I found the idea so bizarre and frightening. He described it as a behavior that often accompanied eating disorders, saying both were self-destructive coping mechanisms.

Jake, Steve, and I all thought her cutting experimentation was brief and in the past, so the night she stretched as I scratched her back, and unknowingly exposed to me the rows of even, perfectly spaced, raw lines on her arms, I was caught completely unprepared. I made an excuse to leave, and taking the steps two at a time, held back my sobs until I was safe behind my closed bedroom door.

Once more, I was the bearer of devastating news for an unsuspecting Steve. "She's cutting herself," I cried, hardly able to catch a breath. "Oh my God, she's cutting herself to shreds." I described the fresh scars; dozens of them, in careful, exact lines. These could not be explained away as an accident. "Who would do that to herself? Why doesn't she see how destructive this is?" Steve had no answers, only painful questions of his own.

The next day I was back on the phone with Kit, who always took the time to reassure me and answer my frantic questions. I was begging for an explanation, hoping for words of wisdom that would account for this type of desperation. Once again, I received the same advice. Don't get into it; let Taryn and Kit work it through.

I'm not the coddling type, but when your child is truly suffering, your heart begins to break off, bit by bit. You tend to offer her those pieces of your heart in hopes that something will assuage the pain—that something, perhaps the pure power of your love, will get through to her. But it wasn't working. As I'd go through my nightly back-scratching ritual with her, I would subtly try to open doors while trying not to see the ugly slashes on her arms. Unable to completely ignore it, I would test the waters. I'd run my fingers over her wounds and ask gentle questions. "What's making you so unhappy?" or "What can I do to help you?" Each time, we'd talk a little, but never get to the core.

I remember one night in particular, when I couldn't stop the tears, and she asked me why I was crying. "I'm crying because of the pain you're obviously feeling," I answered. "I'm crying for you, but also for 'Future Taryn,' when all this is past you, and you glance down and see your scars and are forced to remember. When you're in love, and he looks at your arms and you have to explain and be reminded of how sad you were when you were a teenager." I wanted her to open a window to the future and see it wouldn't always be like this; the scars she was carving into her arms were permanent mementos of a time that someday, she most likely would rather forget.

I had some anger, too. One time there was a cut on my arm, and Taryn, showing obvious curiosity and some concern, asked how it happened. I looked at the cut, and then at her, and without missing a beat, I said, "I did it. I wanted to see what you got from it." I said it without thinking, and as she clearly seemed intrigued by the notion, I quickly said, "No, it's just a cut." I realized I wanted her to feel my pain, but she couldn't—it was a mother's pain, and besides, she felt enough of her own.

Now I knew Taryn was hurting herself on the inside and the outside. And there was nothing I could do to help. It seemed as

long as I could be very busy finding solutions—therapists, facilities, talking to the dance line, researching information—as long
as I was doing everything in my power, I could handle this. Now
nothing was in my power. And I couldn't handle it.

The signs that Taryn was still bulimic could not be denied:
Food was disappearing, cover-up scents were overpowering, and
Taryn's emotional condition was clearly spiraling down. Even
with the layers of clothing, I could see her weight was plum-
meting. I could see it in her arms and her back when I sat with
her at night. It was as if she knew the bulimia was no longer a
secret, so she didn't feel the need to really worry about it. She
was always behind closed doors, and her mood was usually foul
and nasty. At times I would wonder if maybe demons could
possess people—maybe *The Exorcist* wasn't so far off the mark,
because something horrible definitely had ahold of Taryn.

One night, Steve and I headed out for the evening but had to
return for something we'd forgotten. We walked into the kitchen
to find we'd wandered into a full-fledged, all-out binge. Taryn
had ice cream containers, waffle packages, a loaf of bread, and a
myriad of snacks and meal makings spread all over the counter.
We'd only been gone a few minutes! She must have been impa-
tiently counting the seconds until we left!

We looked at her, first in horror, and then with sadness.
Somehow, we smothered our instinct to sweep the whole mess
into the garbage and shake her. Somehow, the lessons learned
materialized in our minds, and like good schoolchildren, we
said, "How can we help you?" And we looked into the eyes of a

demon. This wasn't our daughter. This was the face of evil. She snarled at us, "By getting out of here and leaving me alone." And so we did. We followed the experts' advice and left, visibly shaken by the experience.

And yet other times, she was not just our daughter, but our little girl. She was drowning in turbulence of her own making. She would reach out to us, small, frightened, vulnerable, and unable to understand her own behavior. And sorry. Always sorry for the pain she had caused.

During one of those times, I talked to her about a place we'd heard of while she was at the center. It was a place that took in young women with a variety of issues, from eating disorders to alcoholism to teenage pregnancies. Its focus was spiritual growth, and the girls were encouraged to replace their particular problem with a renewed relationship with God. It didn't charge for its services, and it required a six-month commitment. Furthermore, the girl had to fill out the paperwork, not the family. The girl had to apply, and not all were accepted.

As Taryn progressively seemed worse and worse, I spoke to Kit about it and she checked it out. She agreed that it was an option for Taryn, and since there was a nine-month waiting list after acceptance, it might not be a bad idea for Taryn to at least apply. If she was still in danger at the end of the wait period, she would have options. This particular night, while Taryn was feeling acquiescent, she agreed to apply.

But that did nothing for the immediate situation. I found it all completely overwhelming, and my ability to be happy disintegrated rapidly. I would cry for pretty much no specific reason, and I felt hopeless to do anything about it. As the tears would build up, I'd sometimes journal my anguish, although my words wouldn't always make sense. They were more like bullets of misery.

Hard for her to see disease . . . depression . . . are holding you back from trying to get better. Allowing self to continue with destructive behaviors. . . . No desire to change—happy with what you have. Happy with the eating disorder, happy with being depressed, happy with being lonely—find comfort in the darkness.

My friends were there for me, but it was impossible for them to understand. If you weren't living this nightmare, you couldn't imagine how dark and twisted our world was. My friends could not know the difficulty of instinctively wanting to parent one way and being told to do the exact opposite.

One night at a party, Taryn's second car accident came up in discussion. I was trying to keep things light, even as visions of the crash and the aftermath swept through my mind. One close friend hinted that perhaps tougher consequences at home were in order.

I thought about the officer who had investigated, who had noticed the marks on her arms. I thought about how we couldn't react the way we wanted to because we'd been told not to, and before I knew it, tears were running down my face—tears I couldn't control, no matter how hard I tried. I went outside to compose myself, and although my friends tried to rally around, I finally went home, still crying. I went into my closet, sat on the floor, and sobbed for two hours. I just couldn't stop.

The next day, my friend sent me an e-mail:

> *I'm sorry about last night—I feel like I made you cry and I didn't mean for that to happen at all. Please don't apologize for crying, because I probably would not even leave my house. I admire you and Steve for your strength through all this. We are your friends and are here for you at all times. We continue to pray for Taryn and all of you daily. We love you—Hailey*

In an attempt to try and help her understand our own personal "catch-22," I sent her the following e-mail:

> *Thanks, Hailey, for your lovely note. I know you didn't mean for any of that to happen, and normally I would never have begun the "crying game. . . ."*
>
> *I guess I'm very fragile right now when it comes to Taryn. Unless you're there, it's impossible to imagine just how enormous the impact of this problem can be. . . . To watch your child suffer and*

torture herself in so many little ways, and know you've done every-
thing you can do, is at times so sad you can hardly stand it.

The one thing I want to try to help you understand is that we
can't do more to Taryn than she already does to herself. She already
heaps so much guilt on herself, blames herself for so many things,
and expects so much from herself that it's very counterproductive for
us to punish her and make her feel worse about herself . . . am I going
to get tough on her right now, and "set her straight"? I don't have to.
She beats herself up on a daily basis, and for the life of me, I don't
know why. I'll admit, my instincts are often, like yours, to run a tight
ship and lay down the law. But we've learned, right now with Taryn,
that is not what she needs.

You will go through these teen years, and when Alli and Hunter
are driving and making mistakes, you'll understand more. It doesn't
always work out like you planned. I know you are here for Steve and
me, and I am so thankful for your prayers and friendship. . . . Lorri

Finally, I turned to Kit, hoping to get some reassurances from
her about Taryn's prognosis, and instead, she convinced me to
find my own therapist. Not to learn what to do about Taryn, but
rather, to discover what to do about me. It was a definite low
point, but eventually I would see it as a turning point as well.

Although nothing was going to magically make my problems
go away, Tom was a big help. He didn't try to delve into my
childhood, my parents, or my past. He was interested in what
was going on right now, in the present. He was not interested in
making this a long-term thing. He listened and pointed out

essentials that were obvious and clear to me *after* he said it. He matter-of-factly showed me that the things that were occurring in my life were life-altering and extremely difficult. He made me feel like it was okay and normal to respond the way I was.

"It's called episodic depression," he declared, giving a name to the crying jags, hopelessness, and fatigue that colored most of my days. "I recommend an antidepressant, which will help with these symptoms. It will help you get through this period, and when you've made it through, you won't need them anymore." And there I was. Happy, carefree, contented Lorri . . . on antidepressants. As much as I didn't like the idea of being on drugs, I knew I needed help.

By this time, I had another source of support that was even more help than the antidepressants. For the last few months, I spent several mornings a week walking with my friend, Laurie. Like me, she had a daughter, Amy, who was a junior in high school. Like Taryn, Amy was struggling with a powerful eating disorder. As time passed, our hour-and-a-half walk became a necessary, comforting therapy session.

The girls had differences, but there were so many ways they were the same, and through those similarities, Laurie and I had a common ground. We came to depend on each other in a way no one else could really understand. Even our kind, wonderful husbands were not walking exactly in our shoes. They had their own shoes; the shoes of the fathers of eating disordered daughters. We were the mothers, and our friendship was like a life preserver thrown into the rocky sea.

With Laurie and Wellbutrin helping me, I returned to my "how am I going to fix this" state of mind. Why wasn't this working? What was missing? The only thing I could come up with was the adolescent support group. That was the one arm of recovery recommended by the ranch that we hadn't succeeded in finding. With no local groups available, I once again immersed myself in research: how to start a support group.

Back to the calls, the reading, the conversations. I searched for the right facilitator, someone with whom the girls would feel comfortable, someone who was not just one more doctor to avoid. It took some time, and then I remembered Betsy, the young woman Taryn had spoken with when she'd first returned home. She was someone the girls could relate to—she practically looked the same age. And her own experiences with an eating disorder would make her approachable.

I asked Taryn for her opinion, and she was all for asking Betsy. But Betsy wasn't sure. She was very interested and loved the idea of helping other struggling young women, but the time commitment made her nervous. There was something else holding her back, but I couldn't put my finger on it. In the end, though, she agreed to do it. I was halfway there.

I talked to the ranch and several other facilities about the format for starting a support group, as well as activities and topics for the facilitator to cover. I probably spoke to almost every local health professional and organization that had anything to do with eating disorders to get the word out about the soon-to-be support group for teens. I faxed every middle and high school in the county. Now I had to get the word out to the girls.

I got involved with a group at our high school to bring in a high-energy, nationally recognized educator to speak to the students and parents about the high rate of eating disorders, depression, mood disorders, and other mental and stress-related problems occurring in student populations across the country. He gave a cutting-edge, motivating, and entertaining presentation to the entire student body, and the same night, he appeared to parents from around the county.

It was a worthwhile and highly informative event, and I was proud to be part of it. I felt like I was doing something. At the end of each presentation, the flyers were distributed announcing our new support group for teens, and I felt a sense of relief. Now, hopefully, with this last link, maybe Taryn could muster the courage to beat this monster. Maybe this would be the answer.

The support group began meeting, but it didn't really grow as we had hoped. The adolescent girls expressed interest to Taryn, but to get to the meetings, they had to tell their parents, and most hadn't gotten to that stage. Still, I felt like Taryn at least had Betsy, Amy, and a couple of other girls to talk to once a week in a group. It wasn't much, but it was something.

It unfortunately wasn't enough. Taryn's spiral continued its downward trend, and it swept all of us along with it. And then one day, it became glaringly obvious that my two younger daughters were showing signs of noticeable suffering. That day stands out as one of the worst days of my life. I was already a little down from some episode with Taryn, when my day was interrupted by a phone call.

"Mrs. Benson, this is Taylor's guidance counselor," the carefully modulated voice said through the phone. "Would it be possible for you to come to the school right away? We need to talk to you about Taylor." Oh great. That's what a parent wants to hear. After assuring Mr. Adams that I'd be right in, I called Steve. "It sounds serious," I told him. "You probably should be there, too."

We walked into the school and were ushered into the office of Taylor's counselor. He proceeded to explain that everything was okay, but that one of Taylor's friends had come in and expressed concern for her. "Apparently, she's been talking about suicide," he said quietly. "Can you think of anything at home that might be upsetting her?"

Hmm. I wonder. Steve and I looked at each other in shock. Taylor had never said a word to us, but clearly, our happy-go-lucky, carefree middle daughter was now no longer happy or carefree. Taylor walked into the office, looked at me, then Steve, then Mr. Adams and was at a loss. Why was she here, and more importantly, why were we? She sat down, and the counselor began explaining what had happened. And I watched her eyes fill with tears.

After a brief discussion in the office, I took Taylor home and spent the afternoon hugging her on the couch. We talked for several hours, and it all became painfully clear. Taylor was simply sad. Very, very sad. She had gone through Family Week and come home with very high hopes that her big sister would be better when she returned home. She had thought that Taryn saw what a difficult position she had put Taylor in, and that she would treat her with more kindness now.

Instead, the opposite had happened. Taryn's Jekyll and Hyde mood swings were impossible to predict, and Taylor was still the usual target when the darkness swelled. Worse, Taylor could deny all she wanted, but she knew her sister was worse than ever. And if the best facility in the country hadn't helped her, Taylor feared nothing would. She feared losing her sister, and that fear made her feel sad and hopeless, because Taylor loved Taryn more than she could say.

As we wrapped up our long, involved conversation, Halli came home from elementary school; she was holding a discipline referral slip in her hands and had a stubborn, guilty expression on her face. I stared in disbelief. "A referral?" I asked, incredulously. "Halli, what in the world happened?"

I read the sheet. My sweet ten-year-old apparently didn't like what another girl said to her on the playground, so she slapped her across the face! Bam! All of a sudden, it was crystal clear. Taylor was sad. Halli was angry. It was time to start family therapy. And I was back in my office researching specialists.

As I saw my other two girls suffering, it was hard not to feel resentment toward Taryn. Although I intellectually knew she was also hurting, emotionally I hated what her inability to cope was doing to the rest of us. And of course I couldn't confront her, although my instincts told me to. I could hear the party line playing in my head. "She is harder on herself than we could ever be." So I journaled.

WHAT HAS THIS EATING DISORDER DONE FOR YOU?

Where's the good for you? How does this eating disorder benefit you?

- ruining health, perhaps permanently (maybe no big deal now—things will change)

- has disfigured you, permanently (when you find the perfect guy—and you will—every time he looks at the woman he loves, he will be reminded painfully of your adolescent torture)

- ruining your beauty (no matter what YOU thought, you were so gorgeous—your body, your face, your hair, everything . . . stunning—what drop-dead gorgeous means. Now you're NOT. Your bones stick out—no one thinks that's attractive— NO ONE!! Your hair is falling out, no shine, no luster, nothing. Your face is sallow, sores and redness around your mouth. Who KNOWS what's going on inside of you—it's WAY too scary to go there.

So far, what is this beloved eating disorder doing for you???? Just ruining you. You can't sleep; you're taking drugs (laxatives, diet pills) you know will hurt you. Is this making things better for you?? No. Now you hate school, you're late for EVERYTHING. You miss appointments, late for jobs, don't hear alarms, have no social life. The eating disorder IS your social life.

This has become your excuse for anything gone wrong. "I was doing everything right, and it was too much for me—how, since I was 'perfect,' expectations were high—but that scared me. Now I have an excuse. If I don't do well at what I'm doing, well, how sad, I'm sick, I have an illness. I don't have to maintain my appearance—everyone knows I'm ill, what can they expect from me? I don't really have to try because I'm just so weak from this eating disorder. I don't need friends, I have this eating disorder. . . . Oh no, company is coming—too much to handle, I'll have to eat in front of them, they might watch me."

Never mind that you eat in front of people every day. Never mind that you've done this before. You're off the hook—here's another excuse to give in— "it's too disturbing, I'm SO upset, so I'll just completely freak-out and go overboard. It's okay because it's understood. I have this problem. I can't help it." YOU CAN HELP IT!!!

My anger would spill over the pages like a torrent. And my frustration would build because I had to keep it all to myself. She's hurting, too, I'd tell myself, even as my raging words would spew from my pen. And I'd think, "Now what?"

The support group was in place, we were in family therapy with a terrific psychologist, and I'd done everything I could. She had her team, minus Nancy the nutritionist. Where could we turn now? Steve and I began to feel the shadow of despair.

I came back to school in January determined to be skeletal by summer. It was getting harder and harder to use my parents' scale to weigh myself, so I bought one and hid it underneath a robe in my bathroom closet. I spent hours on a spreadsheet creating a log that I worked on dutifully every day; it had a section for recording the details of my daily exercise, food intake, and spaces to record each of the five daily weigh-ins I required. There was also another section that listed all of the shows relating to eating disorders on television, which I would tape and watch over and over. I decorated the binder making it look colorful and cute; I used my computer to put little scales all over the weigh-in page and little bags of popcorn as the border for the television pages. It is amazing how something so pretty can represent something so ugly.

There was another eating-disordered girl from my neighborhood in my English class. Our mothers were friends who walked together. I remember just sitting staring at her, wishing I could be as skinny as her. In my opinion, at 89 lbs., Amy had the absolute, to-die-for body. I watched her, jealous, wondering what she was doing that I wasn't. She brought an apple, a bottle of water, and a veggie burger in a plastic bag to school every day. So I followed her example, but dropped the apple and added a Diet Coke and prayed I would be her size soon. Ironically enough, she had been someone I had looked up to in the past because she usually ran with the popular crowd; she was one of those girls who seem genetically perfect from birth. I know now that she was suffering just as much as I was, but at the time, I couldn't understand how she could have any worries in her flawless state.

I spent lunch with a couple of other dancers that I had become friends with, including my best friend Kayleigh. I was too embarrassed to eat my 80-calorie, 0-grams-of-fat veggie burger in front of them in the cafeteria, so I would pick it apart during English class, never letting it leave my purse. I remember people giving me odd looks as I slowly ate the patty, piece by piece. I spent lunch with Kayleigh, talking about clothes and how many calories were in cranberry juice.

Kayleigh would come over every now and then and we would drink cheap rum in my bedroom and smoke pot on the roof. Or we would sneak out at night and drink wine coolers on the beach, listening to the ocean and talking about God. I slowly pushed everyone else out of my life, but she was the one I held on to; she was confident, attractive, and funny—everything I wanted to be. Somehow being close to her made me feel like I could somehow become more like her.

We became a strange mix between the best friends seen in teen movies and partners in crime. Our relationship was purely symbiotic: she needed me because I could get cigarettes and booze from friends at work, and I needed her because she was my only connection to what high school was supposed to be. We would talk about everything and laugh together, drunk on Smirnoff Ice. Our relationship made me happy.

Unfortunately, it was the only thing that made me happy. My life was getting worse. I would stare at the mirror for hours and pick myself apart, killing any shred of self-esteem I had left. Kayleigh switched into a different lunch period, so I lied to the rest of the girls and said I had to be tutored during lunch. Instead, I spent the break in the bathrooms, making deep, even cuts along the inside of my arms. I checked out every book the school library had on eating disorders and would read them as I listened to the girls chatting as they gossiped and laughed between classes and lunch. I hated them because they seemed so happy, and I hated myself because I couldn't be happy. So I carried my scissors around in my purse for comfort instead of friends. I never knew when the time would come when I would need to bring the piercing blade to my pale skin.

In January I caused a major car accident. I made a left turn and slammed into the person driving on the road parallel to the one I was trying to turn onto. Luckily no one was hurt, but both cars were destroyed and I was humiliated and upset. I sobbed uncontrollably during the entire event; luckily the police officers that showed up were very understanding and sympathetic. I was not cited for the accident, but something much more humiliating happened. As everything was being wrapped up, one of the cops came over to check me for airbag burns. Before I could stop him he had pushed back my sleeves. He stared at my sliced-up arms for a few moments, shocked and confused, and then suddenly let go and shook his head to himself as he walked away.

I wanted to scream. The look of horror on the cop's face as he examined my arms was too much for me. The attention I had once craved so badly was becoming overwhelming and embarrassing. The accident happened right outside the building where my dad worked, so I ran inside and into the bathroom. I leaned up against the wall, crying uncontrollably; I dug through my purse furiously and finally found my treasure. Trying desperately to hold my hand steady I dug the blade into my skin and ripped open my arm. Blood gushed out and mixed with the last of my salty tears as I finally calmed down for a minute. Everything was suddenly okay again. Except now I needed stitches, which I knew I would never get.

The next day the school deputy called me down to his office. Apparently the cop who had examined my arms at the accident had told him about the cuts on my arm. He wanted to make sure I was okay and that I was getting help. I sat in the chair reliving the humiliation from the day before, nodding and trying not to cry. The meeting was short, but the rest of the day I walked around the halls of my school wondering who else knew.

Things weren't much better at home. I had lost all desire to hide my raging bulimia and would stay up all night bingeing on my parents' food and puking in my bathroom. The entire upstairs of the house smelled like the cheap perfume I sprayed everywhere to cover up the smell of puke, and underneath my bed became a little gro-cery store. I would stock up on food in my car and sneak it in once my family went to bed; that way I could just sit upstairs in my room every day after school and binge and purge.

My eating habits fluctuated; I would try to starve for a while, but inevitably go back to bingeing. I binged and purged up to six or seven times a day. It consumed me. I would binge on the way to school and purge when I got there. It would happen again during lunch break. Twice before dinner, once after dinner, and once or twice in the evening, depending on how long I could stay awake. It began to take over my life. It was all I thought about—what I lived for. I no longer had any boyfriends or friends except Kayleigh.

I was afraid of what I would do to anyone who got in my way. My parents or sisters would walk in on my bingeing every now and then. I became a monster; screaming, threatening, throwing things to get them to leave their own house to let me binge in peace. My sisters usu-ally got the most of it because there was a limit to what I could say to my parents, but I would lash out at anyone who tried to stop me. I was violent and angry as I binged; I was a demon with an appetite. And an addiction.

I would lay in bed with my little sister, Halli, at night sometimes, scratching her back and holding her before she fell asleep. She would tell me how much she loved me and how much she worried. I could see the pain in her ten-year-old eyes, and I promised to do bet-ter. I told her that I barely purged anymore and that she shouldn't worry because everything was going to be okay. "But you are so skinny now," she would counter, which brought tears to my eyes. All of her pleading didn't make me stop; in fact, the guilt it caused made me want to binge more.

I knew my mother was desperate. She was noticeably upset often and the tension was always high between us. Needless to say, I wasn't surprised when she told me she was creating a support group for me, the girl in my English class, and whoever else would come. She orchestrated a nationally renowned presenter to come to my high school, and hung up a flyer in my ballet studio. Unfortunately, the only people that ever came were me, Amy, and my friend Jaime. I felt bad because my mother had put so much work into it, but I didn't really mind because I loved listening to Amy and Betsy's stories. It had the adverse effect that my mother thought it would, and afterward I always spiraled into huge, uncontrollable binges. I was like a child who sat around and talked about candy all day with her friends, so the rush of actually getting to eat the candy was amazing.

During my stay in the rehab center, one of my good friends had told me about a different place that also treated girls with eating disorders. It was free of charge if you were accepted, it catered to many issues instead of solely eating disorders, and it heavily emphasized spirituality. Unfortunately there were a lot of applicants; girls sometimes spent years on the waiting list, if they ever got in at all. I told my mother about it sometime while I was still away, and sometime around February she started bringing it up again. I applied begrudgingly so that she would leave me alone. I figured maybe if I applied, she would stop bugging me about cleaning the bathroom or eating all the ice cream. It was never meant to be an actual solution; I never counted on actually getting accepted.

CHAPTER ELEVEN

God Grant Me the Serenity

March to June 2004

Something had to change. I knew I needed to stop worrying about Taryn and start worrying about me, but it was easier said than done. We were all very aware that Taryn was living in her own disordered, terrible world. And it was becoming quite clear that there was nothing we could do about it. Every effort had been made and she was making no progress at all.

Our family therapist, Paul, was terrific. After a few sessions with him, some things became apparent. Our family was basically okay, better than okay. "Your family is great," he told us. "You love each other and communicate well, and your rules are clear and fair. The problem is you have a family member who has an eating disorder and is suffering, and you're all feeling it."

While his observation didn't solve anything, at least I knew that at the core, all wasn't lost. He made us feel better as parents.

And he thought Taylor was fine. Perhaps lacking in some self-esteem, but healthy overall. That also was a relief. Halli was the only one who didn't want to go to the sessions because she had a tough time describing her feelings. Paul felt it was an age-appropriate reaction and didn't think we needed more than a couple of all-family sessions.

Instead we'd meet in groups of two or three, and since Taryn seemed to connect with him, we added Paul to her personal team. He was a great source of reassurance in my search for normalcy.

About this time, a letter arrived. Taryn was accepted into a faith-based program in Tennessee and was on the waiting list. This became the panacea on which I pinned all my hopes. The philosophy of the program was based on a completely different approach from everything we'd tried to date, and since I was starting to see the bulimia as an evil force, it made sense that maybe a spiritual tactic might be more effective than anything else.

She seemed less than enthused about "making the cut," but at the same time, she was fairly faithful about the work required before entrance. Because there was no charge for the treatment, and there was a long wait to get in, the facility wanted to make sure that the applicants were serious about wanting recovery. Each month that passed between their acceptance and their admission, the candidates received books to read and then were required to report on their reaction. Taryn did the work without complaint.

I couldn't read her. I took comfort in the fact that she'd applied and was now doing the monthly work. Grasping at straws, I would hope that some part of her was ambivalent, that even if it was deep inside, there was a shred of a desire to recover. On the other hand, her behavior spoke volumes, and while I really had no idea how entrenched she was in the disorder, it was clear that she had no intention of crawling out of her hole yet. It was as though she thought she could take full advantage of her wait time and then magically lose the eating disorder when she went to Tennessee.

Even as I searched for my own path to acceptance, there were times when I was consumed with anger at Taryn's refusal to see what she was doing to herself. I wrote in frustration.

Where is the character you were BORN with; where is the morality you were taught; where is the I CAN attitude you've shown your whole life? No one can fix this for you. NO ONE but you. Now you think, "Oh good, they'll fix it . . . I can keep doing all my SHIT and then fix it when I go there."

Only it won't get fixed. It will stay there. It will be seven to nine months MORE ingrained in you, and seven to nine months harder to get rid of . . . if YOU don't do something YOURSELF, you will see just how hideous this disorder is.

You have just this one life—you control it, YOU decide what it will be. And you are currently sabotaging all your options. Where once there was potential for greatness, soon you'll be lucky to get mediocrity. Your options will slip away. If you don't soon start looking at yourself how God looks at you, being pleased with the gifts you've been given, allow yourself the forgiveness that everyone has already given you, it will be too late. Damage will be done.

By the way, you're not fooling anyone. We all know. We know when you're lying; we know when you're doing your sickening thing. Where you deserve admiration, you will get pity. Is that REALLY what you are seeking in life????

Although my journaling was colored by my frustration, and like Taryn, I would never say out loud most of what I wrote, I ached to say some of the things I thought were so true. My instincts told me it could actually do her good to hear some tough love rhetoric, and I was sick of following the party line and staying somewhat detached. I was too afraid, however, to stray far from the virtual playbook we'd been given. I lived in fear that I would say or do something that could affect her progress. The only thing was . . . what progress?

My therapist, Tom, was the first to point out a series of truths that made me start to see the futility of thinking I could greatly impact Taryn's recovery. "How do you know she's writing the truth?" he asked me one day, during a discussion about my reading the terrible entries in her journal. "She knows you've read it in the past. She could easily be trying to push your buttons by intentionally writing things she knows will send you into a tailspin."

I couldn't argue with that. Taryn wasn't above that kind of manipulation. In fact, I had been dealing with that kind of manipulation for over a year. Suddenly, there was no reason for me to read her journals anymore. It didn't matter what was in them, because I couldn't know that any of it was based on reality.

He also made me see that I could hold family dinners, hide food, follow her around, or do any number of things to try to prevent her from continuing her eating disorder, but could I really accomplish anything if she honestly wasn't interested in stopping? This didn't make me completely give up trying, but it started me on my path to put myself back together. My producer mentality kicked back in—if I couldn't make Taryn's problems go away, maybe I could fix my own.

I began to look to faith myself. So many little things, little miracles, had been occurring over the last year, showing me I wasn't alone. Although I felt like my faith was being tested, I was led back by two main forces. One was a special priest and friend who constantly amazed me with his uncanny way of saying just what I needed to hear. He taught me to "breathe, smile, and relax," a meditation technique that really did work to get me through difficult moments.

I would drag myself into church, beaten up by something that had happened, and his sermon would be completely related and full of ways to let go and move on. Father Jerry never failed to come through with something to help me get through the next week, and his messages began to do more—they started to help me let go.

The second force that helped me make sense of what was happening was a book Jake had spoken about during Family Week called *The Purpose Driven Life*. For reasons I didn't understand, I felt moved to read it. It changed my outlook immeasurably.

Instead of focusing all my energies on how to "fix" Taryn and her problems, and feeling betrayed and sorry for myself, the book's messages forced me to begin to look at life differently. I started to see this as my journey, a journey with challenges that I was meant to face. I realized that everyone is on their own trip, and no one gets through without pain, suffering, grief, and lessons learned the hard way. If it's not trouble with our children, it's our spouse, or aging parents, or addictions, financial worries, or something.

As obvious as this may be to some people, it was a revelation for me. I felt betrayed that I'd followed the rules and this had happened. Maybe it was naive, but I believed that if I did the right thing, my life would go smoothly. This new realization helped me let go of that sense of betrayal. It made it possible to see that this wasn't actually even about me.

More importantly, I finally was able to accept that Taryn was on *her* journey, her own excursion, fraught with the challenges *she* was meant to face. My viewpoint changed, and I began to be able to let go. I felt ready to let her face her own demons without my feeling somehow responsible to stop it. It was a tremendous turning point, and it allowed me to feel like Steve and I had truly done all we could. Before I knew it, I didn't need the antidepressants anymore, and I weaned myself off them.

Of course, I did not turn into Deepak Chopra overnight. While I had gained some tremendous insight, the fact remained that my beloved daughter was still in deep trouble, was potentially doing some major damage to herself, and didn't seem to be making any progress psychologically. It was impossible to know what she was really thinking, and we didn't believe much of what she told us anymore. Her actions spoke loudly, however, and she wasn't making a huge effort to cover up what she was or wasn't doing.

Although I was beginning to work on my own stress management, it was still a miserable time. Steve and I discussed how to do things in our power, to try to lessen Taryn's effect on our lives. We tried everything from hiding food, not buying food, policing more, trying to make it her responsibility—anything and everything. We decided we were not going to supply her binge food, well aware she'd just spend her own hard-earned money on it. Knowing it wasn't fair to restrict snacks and sweets from everyone else, but not wanting to tempt Taryn, we would hide them all over the house. But it didn't matter; she'd just find other ways, and the bulimia still ruled over us all.

Since my sophomore year, I had wanted to graduate early. High school was far too literally the bane of my existence and, as usual, I just knew a major change like going to college would suddenly perfect me. College was somewhat similar to losing fifteen pounds—I would blossom overnight into a beautiful, skinny model of perfection in every way, shape, and form and have billions of friends.

This desire still enveloped me; however, my situation was a little less than ideal for a college freshman. My bulimia was still completely out of control, and I hadn't lessened any of my other self-destructive behaviors either. By applying to the faith-based program, I thought it would give my mother reason to believe that I wanted to recover. I also applied to the University of Florida. I got in to both.

I was in shock when I got the phone call telling me I was accepted to the rehab program. It actually made me happy because it proved I was really sick; they wouldn't waste their limited time and space on just anybody. I still never planned on going into the program, though; it was still simply a ploy so I could start college. Reluctantly, I continued with all the projects on the waiting list—reading different books and writing about them—all the while praying I would just stay on that list forever.

I was obsessed with pro–eating disorder sites and would often look to them for tricks and tips. One site had a link to an article about the different types of eating disorders, and it included a type of disorder that involved eating nonfood items, including artificial sweeteners. It seemed like it would be worth a try because it would satisfy my sweet tooth and slow down my bingeing.

Sneaking downstairs, I would fill the deep pockets of my robe with Splenda packets. I would rip open the packets and eat the contents while I read or did homework. It was like eating pure sugar, and soon my bingeing and purging rate was halved because I replaced it with Splenda binges.

Unfortunately, Splenda was really expensive. And since I was eating hundreds of packets a day, I needed a way to buy them in bulk. I would steal or borrow my mom's Costco card and buy massive amounts of the sweetener. I would smile and explain to the other customers who asked about my bizarre purchases that I used the Splenda for cooking, giving baking tips to the little old ladies.

My mother caught me a few times, and I knew it was awkward, but Splenda provided such an ideal solution that it seemed stupid to stop. I started bringing bags of it to school and eating it instead of lunch, curled up in a bathroom stall. My weight began to drop more and more since I was barely eating, and Kit threatened me with the hospital. I would count my ribs as I lay in bed at night, rubbing my hands across my collar bone and my protruding hip bones. I loved the way they felt.

The Splenda habit eventually became too difficult to hide and too expensive to support; even though I was buying it in bulk, it was still very costly. I never had any extra money because I spent everything that I earned on cigarettes and Splenda. I turned back to bingeing and purging and put on a few pounds, satisfying my therapist.

I felt completely out of control. Within weeks of dropping the Splenda habit, I was bingeing so often that the waitstaff at a local breakfast joint knew me by name because I came in daily. I had to alternate which grocery stores I went to because I usually went more than once a day. I was running out of money again and my parents had gone back to hiding food.

Purging was also becoming more difficult. My gag reflex was creeping farther and farther back down my throat, and occasionally I would be physically unable to purge. One of these times, I was working in the same office that my dad worked. The company had hired me to help out around the office, and one of the jobs I did was scan documents into a computer network. Since this job required me to work alone in a corner cubicle, often uninterrupted for hours, I would bring a backpack full of food and binge and purge through my shift.

One morning I was working, eating, and surfing pro–eating disorder websites. Unfortunately, when I went to the bathroom, I just couldn't throw up. I tried everything for nearly a half hour: sticking my fingers down my throat, coughing as hard as I could—I even used a pen to try to reach my gag reflex. I finally had to go back to my station, afraid someone would find me missing. My face was bright red and bloated, and I could hardly swallow; big salty tears ran down my face from the stress. I didn't know what to do—it was horrible and I was desperate.

I ran downstairs and asked my boss for an early lunch, telling her something about a doctor's appointment that I had forgotten to mention. She was so sweet and patted me on the back as I hurried out the door, humiliated by my bulging stomach. I drove to the nearest pharmacy and ran inside, searching the aisles desperately. Finally, I gave up looking and went up to the pharmacist.

"Excuse me," I waved at the pharmacist, pulling out an old receipt I had stuffed in my pocket. "My mom sent me in here to pick up something and I couldn't find it. It's called eepicack or ipicock," I pretended to read off the receipt. The pharmacist nodded.

"Ipecac. Little ones at home?" he said with a smile. I nodded and went on and on about how the baby was starting to walk as he packaged up the small bottle. I paid quickly and ran into the bathroom, drinking the contents as soon as I was safe inside a stall.

It hit me a lot faster than I expected. I became dizzy and nauseated and held on to the top of the toilet for support. I couldn't stand up, my knees buckled, and I collapsed into the toilet, vomiting violently over and over until there was nothing left but bile. I stayed in the bathroom for an hour, staring at the mess and trying to regain my grasp on reality. Finally I got up, flushed the toilet, washed my face and hands, and headed back to work with the world still swirling around my head.

CHAPTER TWELVE

A Line in the Sand

June to August 2004

Suddenly, Taryn's junior year in high school was over. We had made it through somehow, and I felt a little like I'd been through boot camp. It wasn't just her eating disorder, although that was certainly the most unbearable. When she isolated herself in her room, we encouraged her to go out with friends. When she finally went out with friends, we became nervous about what she was doing. Although she was a master of disguise, and there were never overt signs of drinking or drug use, we knew something was up.

When she'd come home at night, we had a rule that she come and give us a kiss good night. As many wise parents know, it's a nice tradition, and it also gives the parent a chance to sniff out the results of an evening's fun. She always passed the test. Still, my mother's intuitive alarms were often clanging as she left our room.

It was a difficult paradox. When she was holed up in her room, writing dark, frightening poetry or designing another revealing collage, we worried that Taryn was descending into a solitary, lonely hell. But when she was out, mostly with Kayleigh, we were uneasy and concerned for her safety. But at least those fears were more in line with typical worries for parents of teenagers. We just had no idea, as usual, of the frequency and seriousness of her "fun." Taryn was extremely gifted at keeping us in the dark.

I caught her sneaking out a couple of times because I would just sit up in bed during a sound sleep, with a "feeling." I would walk around and look outside for her car, which was always there and not an indication at all if she was home or not. Up the stairs I'd go, and . . . no Taryn. That meant sitting up waiting, calling her cell phone to let her know she'd been busted, and then doling out a punishment upon her return.

It was disappointing each time we discovered Taryn had made another bad choice. Although we knew that all kids made mistakes, at the time, a little voice inside would say, "Why would she do this? We talked about this—she knows better." It seemed it was always something with her. But again, I knew I wasn't the only parent fighting these battles. It was the anorexia and bulimia that carried the big stick in this war of wills.

As summer approached, Taryn pleaded to go visit her cousin in Ohio. She was insistent that things would be better there. It was similar to her belief that if she could just get out of high school and into college, her life would suddenly and magically change.

This did not seem like a great idea to me. We were still in an emotional war zone, and the idea of Taryn bringing her strange and often disgusting behavior into someone else's house had all kinds of wrong written over it. I had no idea how to really prepare Steve's brother and sister-in-law for what might occur. I could hardly stand it when I would walk past her room and smell that perfumey cover-up odor that sickened me. How could someone else understand? How could someone else, who hadn't been through this, know what to say, or more importantly, what not to say?

In the end, we let her go. I wish I could say it was because we believed her, or because we thought it would make a difference. I guess we hoped it would. But if we were going to be honest, it was probably more because we were tired. We were tired of walking on eggshells, patrolling at night, holding our tongues, worrying if there would be another shocking discovery or more grisly marks on her body. We needed a break from wondering if her heart would stop, or if more capillaries in her eyes would burst, or if she'd gotten hold of more laxatives or diet pills.

We were sick of seeing little, raw cuts in the corners of her mouth and telltale sores on the third knuckle of her hand. Where she was once extremely careful about hiding everything and leaving no clues, she now seemed to live in her own world with her own rules. And while I would sometimes get angry at what she was doing to us, I would just as often feel afraid and helpless at what was happening to my child.

I remembered nights when, after tucking in the other girls, I would go into Taryn's room and wonder if this would be the night when I'd discover she wasn't breathing. And nights when I would just cry because I had no idea how this whole thing was going to end. So, I called my sister-in-law, Shirley, and told her what I thought she could expect, and angel that she was, she assured me that she still wanted Taryn to come. So we let her go.

Once she was winging her way north, that familiar feeling of relief washed over me. When she had been in treatment, that feeling of relief was offset by a terrible hole in my heart. I missed her so much it hurt. This time, the past six months had taken its toll. That part of my heart with the hole in it was gone. It had been ripped off and torn to shreds, and now I needed a break from the pain, the worry, the fear.

I did worry about Taryn's aunt and uncle, though. How would they handle the indescribable strangeness that we knew would surely accompany Taryn on her visit? I think her Aunt Shirley probably thought a few good meals would get Taryn back on track. That's what most people thought—those who hadn't lived with an anorectic or bulimic. I remember one relative couldn't understand why we didn't just make her eat. Why didn't we sit with her and force her to eat and keep it down? This relative was a doctor. Go figure.

We began our annual summer trek back to Colorado, where Taryn would join us after her visit. It was during that drive at the end of June when I got an unexpected phone call. It was Helen from the faith-based program. They had an early opening for Taryn. August 10.

It is hard to explain the sensations that ran through me with the news. Hope was certainly one emotion. More like desperate hope, because this truly was the last chance. If this program didn't work, there were no more new options. It had to work.

I also experienced disbelief, because it was hard to imagine that my daughter was going to go to another facility, this time for six months. I had hoped that it would never come to that, that she would figure it all out and be well, long before the nine- to twelve-month waiting period would be over. It was just a little over five months since she applied, and she was worse than ever. She had to go.

At the same time, I was excited for Taryn to have this opportunity. How lucky that we'd heard of this place. How fortunate that she'd been chosen to go. What a blessing that an opening had been created so soon, because the way things were going, I knew she'd be that much deeper in the disease as time passed.

I definitely also felt dread, because I knew Taryn wouldn't be happy to hear the date had been moved up. In my mind, she looked at this as a someday thing—something a little surreal. Sure, she'd applied, apparently to assuage our anxiety and get us off her back. Clearly not because she wanted to get better. It seemed her place on the waiting list was like a get-out-of-jail-free card to her. She could completely immerse herself in her disorder, and sometime down the road, far in the future, this place would fix her. Only the place was beckoning now. And my gut told me Taryn was not ready to be "fixed." I did not look forward to her hearing the big news.

I was right. Taryn was furious when she got the call. "I'm not going," she insisted, the next time we talked. "I have everything all planned out, and I don't want to go until after the holidays— that's when it was supposed to happen." We knew her plan was to finish high school by Christmas, do the program the following six months, and enter college with her class the next fall. She did not intend to deviate from that plan, even when I explained that she could lose her place on the waiting list if she didn't take the August spot. "It's not fair," she wailed, "and I'm not doing it!"

Oh good. Now we could look forward to a big battle when she came to Colorado. I let Nashville know that we had some things to work through, but we fully intended on her taking the opening. Since this was supposed to be all about the patient wanting recovery and voluntarily taking the steps to attain it, we didn't mention that one of the things we had to work through was how to make her go.

In the meantime, Ohio wasn't proving to be the magic potion that Taryn thought it would be. Her life wasn't turning around and her problems weren't dissolving away. Although her aunt tried her hardest to include Taryn and come up with activities for her, her sad niece spent a lot of time on the computer in the basement and was up at all hours of the night, unable to relax or sleep.

My time off was coming to a close. Taryn was arriving in Colorado, and Steve and I drove to Denver to pick her up at the airport. The whole three-hour drive, we discussed and diagrammed our plan of attack. We came up with a list of pros and cons regarding an August 10 entry in the Nashville program.

And we really thought about how far we were willing to go to get our life back.

We realized that this opportunity was not only for her—it was for our whole family. We couldn't all remain in this hopeless mire forever. If something didn't change, Steve and I were afraid everything we held dear would be in jeopardy, and we were not willing to risk that anymore. When our oldest daughter walked off the plane, we were ready with our ultimatum. We found a place to sit down and delivered it.

"Taryn, we've decided we will not live this way anymore," we told her as calmly as we could. "We won't expose the other girls to this sickness anymore, and we don't think you can beat this on your own." We then went through all of her arguments with our pro and con list, illustrating how going to Tennessee would greatly enhance her chances of recovering and getting her life back. It was clearly the choice with the most options.

We then went over her choices if she didn't go to the program. She could stop the eating disorder cold turkey. Or, and we both inwardly shuddered as we lowered the boom, if she wasn't ready to recover, she would have to find another place to live. "We can't do this for you," we told her. "We can only control how we will or won't live. The decision is yours."

She seemed a little taken aback at having the responsibility placed in her lap. We outlined the math Steve had done to come up with what it would cost for her to be on her own. We were both surprised when she didn't really get angry or come back with her own ammunition. It was as if she'd already come to the same conclusion. "I know I have to go," she admitted. "I didn't want to go so soon, but I guess I'm going to have to."

We silently sighed in relief. We hugged her and told her we loved her. We told her we were behind her 100 percent, and we'd always be there for her. We told her we hoped our reunion in Colorado would be a time of comfort, family fun, and good memories. Then we headed back to Steamboat Springs, feeling that maybe, just maybe, we were on the same page. But it wasn't over. We weren't even in the same book.

Taryn wasn't going to go quietly off to treatment. She was going to have a last hurrah. She responded with behavior that basically said, "This is it—let's make the most of my time before I go." Her eating habits hadn't changed, and she was always going off for "walks." Naturally, we always thought the worst. And then, one night when she and Taylor returned from an outing of "looking for shooting stars," I was sure I smelled smoke.

They had been sitting on a blanket on the mountain behind our place, and I found the blanket in the morning and smelled it. You couldn't miss the scent—it wasn't like Taryn to leave such an obvious clue behind. When Taylor woke up, I used one of my usually successful interrogation techniques.

"Taylor, I know Taryn's smoking, but I didn't think she would do it with you around," I began. "I'm very upset that last night she smoked in front of you." She looked at me quizzically and asked, "Why do you think that?" Giving her my best "You can't fool me" glance, I replied, "I could smell the smoke on her, and this morning I could smell it on the blanket."

"She doesn't usually smoke in front of me," Taylor said, clearly trying to defend her sister. "We were just out for a long time last night. Don't be mad at her." But I was. I had my confirmation. Once again, I could hardly believe that Taryn would be stupid enough to smoke. This from someone who, as a child, would point out people who were smoking and whisper, horrified, "Mom look—they're SMOKING!"

Smoking was a bit of a pet peeve for me, mostly because I just couldn't understand the allure. It seemed dirty, smelly, and gross, with the added bonus of causing cancer. How could Taryn, with her addictive personality, and knowing all the dangers and negatives, take up a habit so difficult to stop?

When Taryn got up that morning, she immediately said she was going to walk down to Starbucks and read for a little while. I decided I was going to look for proof so we could discuss it when she returned. It wasn't hard to find it. Under her bed was a black bag with several bags and boxes of binge food, and a CARTON of cigarettes. Not a pack, a carton! I was furious. I walked into our bedroom and showed my find to Steve.

Steve, who had smoked for a time in his life, was not as appalled as I was, or as surprised. "She'll quit," he said with confidence. "She's just experimenting." I wasn't so sure, but in any case, I wondered what to do with the unopened carton. We decided to just return it to the store and let it be an expensive lesson for her. We were curious how she would react—whether she'd confront us or just say nothing.

We didn't have long to wait. As soon as she returned from her walk, we told her we wanted to talk to her. "Taryn, we know you've been smoking," Steve said, since we'd mutually decided he should be the bearer of this bad news. Of course she denied it, finally admitting that maybe every once in a while she might smoke. "It calms me down," she said. That's when I brought out my big gun. "We found a carton, Taryn," I revealed. "That's a lot of cigarettes to buy when you only smoke one every now and then."

Out came the defiance and anger. "What did you do with it?" she demanded. "That belongs to me!" We were amazed by her chutzpah. No more denials—she went right to indignation. "Are you kidding me?" I asked her in disbelief. "You're seventeen! You're not legally allowed to buy or have cigarettes, not to mention we are going to do everything in our power to stop you from smoking!"

"Where are they?" she screamed again. We told her we disposed of them. We explained that we knew she would find ways to smoke if she wanted to, but we would continue searching and throw away any cigarettes we found. If there was anything we could do to prevent her from starting a deadly habit, we were going to do it.

We told her we were disappointed—that for a smart girl, this was one stupid thing to start doing. "For heaven's sake," I said, "You know how addictive cigarettes are—why would you even toy with something like that?" But she had already started to shut down. She was mad and just wanted the discussion to be over.

That afternoon, Steve and I drove to the local airport to pick up a favorite relative, and we were looking forward to a fun evening with the family. When we got home, there was a big welcome and everyone visited for a while before heading off to get ready for the evening. I went into my bathroom to wash up and then started around the corner to where the shower, toilet, and tub were located. Although there were no lights on, something made me stop short. Something was not right, but I didn't know what it was.

And then I discovered just how angry Taryn was at us. She obviously wanted to display the most horrendous act of defiance she could think of to retaliate against our authority. What was the worst thing she could do to us? She did it in our shower. When I flipped on the lights and saw, with horror, the hate that Taryn was capable of dishing out to us, I was paralyzed for a moment.

She knew how traumatized we all were by her eating disorder. She was well aware of how this would affect Steve and me. I turned away and just stood there, not knowing what to do. The feelings washing over me were like nothing I'd ever felt before. Taryn had never been aggressive toward us in her whole life. She may have had some attitude, and she'd certainly given us a run for our money the last couple years, but it never seemed overtly hateful or directed intentionally at us. This was both.

Because her anorexia and bulimia were at the root of all the torment we'd been experiencing, I saw the enormous and vile spread of vomit in our shower as a symbol of her total disregard of our feelings—a deliberate and calculated attempt to hurt us at the deepest level. And I was cut to the core. It took everything I had to call Steve into our room with a normal voice.

He was furious. While I disintegrated into a sobbing heap, my normally calm husband seethed. "She knows how cruel this is," he spit out. "This was the worst thing she could think of to do to us." It was true, but what now? What was the therapeutically correct thing to say and do? Did it matter? How should a parent respond to such malicious and spiteful behavior? We sat holding each other and tried to figure out how we would handle this latest outrage. Then we called her in.

She came into the room, insolent and with a hostile look in her eye. She was ready to do battle. We, however, were not. With quiet but deadly calm voices, we took turns delivering our message. "What you did was unspeakably cruel and hateful. All we've done is love you, support you, be here for you, and try to protect you. With everything we've been through, that's all we've tried to do. For you to take your anger out on us in this way is so completely unacceptable, and so hurtful, that we're not sure how we will forgive you."

Taryn started in about how we had no right to take her property, but Steve cut her off. "We had every right. This is our house and you are our daughter, and our job is to protect you. But even so, no matter how mad you were, this was a vicious and totally inappropriate response. We have been too good to you for you to treat us like this."

It may have been the tone of Steve's voice or the stricken look on my face, but Taryn looked like she realized that she had stepped way over the line. She stopped talking. "You will have to go in and clean up that mess in the bathroom right now," I told her. "And then you'll have to figure out how to apologize to us and make this better. I'm not sure how you'll do that, and I'm not sure how we'll forgive you. I'm not sure about anything right now."

Taryn didn't even argue. She just got up and cleaned the bathroom.

The next day, I checked my e-mail and found the following message from Taryn.

THERE ONCE WAS A GIRL
WHO DIDN'T KNOW WHAT SHE WANTED
SO SHE SET OFF TO FIND IT
SHE BATTLED, TOILED, AND HUNTED

BUT SHE STARTED TO LOOK
IN ALL THE WRONG PLACES;
TOO MANY BAD CHOICES
TOO MANY SCARY FACES

SHE MADE MANY MISTAKES
AND OF NONE IS SHE PROUD
BUT SHE MADE UP HER MIND
AND SHOUTED OUT LOUD:

"I NEVER ASKED FOR YOUR PAIN
I NEVER ASKED FOR YOUR TEARS
BUT ALL I WANT IS FORGIVENESS
AND YOUR HELP TO COMFORT MY FEARS

I'M STARTING A JOURNEY
TO WHERE—I DON'T KNOW
BUT I NEED YOUR LOVE 'CAUSE
WITHOUT IT I HAVE NO WILL TO GO

SO, PLEASE, IF YOU CAN
JUST LOVE ME AGAIN,
I MISS YOU MORE THAN YOU KNOW
AND I NEED YOU TO HOLD MY HAND

ALTHOUGH THEY SAID
THAT LOVE IS PATIENT AND KIND
THEY HAD NO IDEA
HOW HARD THAT IS TO FIND

SO THERE'S NOTHING LEFT TO SAY
NO MORE TIME TO REGRET,
CAN YOU TRY TO FORGIVE ME—
EVEN THOUGH WE'LL NEVER FORGET?"

i am so sorry . . . for everything . . . you really mean the world to me and i was at the end of my rope . . . i wasn't thinking and i just cracked . . . i let my anger take over and forgot how much i love you . . . but most importantly, i was a selfish, disgusting, cruel idiot, and i don't deserve your love or your forgiveness—but if you can find it in your heart, please forgive me . . . I know I'm not perfect and i will never be—but i love you so much and i miss your hugs and back-scratches (well, duh), and smiles . . . you don't have to send this to 200 people or anything like those wacky chain letters . . . but if you could just tell me that you love me—despite all my mistakes—i

promise i'll try a million times harder to be the daughter you want
me to be.

i love you and i am so sorry.

Taryn

She had found a way to apologize, and as I read it with tears running down my face, I knew she'd made it possible for me to forgive her. There was no getting around it. Taryn needed what the Nashville center was offering.

She seemed resigned to her early entry into round two of treatment. I knew she was disappointed to change her college plans again, as she'd already changed them once. She had applied to the University of Florida (UF) earlier in the year and had been accepted based on three years of high school—no small feat. Since she was clearly struggling, and a second inpatient stay loomed on the horizon, we persuaded her to defer her entrance until January, and now this would change things. I hoped she might start to realize that the eating disorder was starting to dictate her life to her. It was in charge of her.

We arrived back in Florida just days before Taryn's impending departure. As the hours clicked away, her reluctance to go grew. She told me she was nervous about the whole religious philosophy behind the treatment, because her faith at that point was shaky at best. When I heard that, my anxiety level skyrocketed.

I expected that the spiritual aspect of the program was going to be of a more fundamentalist nature than our religion. While being a born-again Christian wasn't a prerequisite for acceptance, it was definitely the main focus. I was willing to risk that she might turn away from Catholicism and embrace what they were preaching. If it helped her overcome the bulimia, however, I didn't care which church she ended up joining.

But now she almost sounded like an agnostic. This wasn't going to work unless she accepted the agenda; unless she gave in, gave up, and stopped clinging to the eating disorder. This place was going to ask her to cling to God instead, and now she was telling me she wasn't even sure she believed in God. We needed a miracle.

The Sunday before she left, we got it. After an irrational and nasty exchange about her negative attitude, the family went to church and sat separately—Taryn sitting with the youth group. We all sat rather sullenly until it occurred to every one of us simultaneously—all three readings either used food analogies or literally were about food. I was already tearing up just hearing the readings. Then Father Jerry started his sermon.

It seemed that every other word had a food connotation—being hungry, needing the bread of life, being fed by God. Then he began to tell a true story about a woman with miraculous oranges. It was so direct and full of applicable references that he might as well have started the sermon saying, "Taryn, this one's for you." I had tears running down my face, and near the end of his talk, Taryn stood up and quickly jogged out the back door, her face wet as she sobbed. I ran out after her, and she fell into my arms.

"Mom, he was talking to me," she cried. And my heart

skipped a beat. She had heard it. The first miracle was his homily. The second was that she hadn't been lost in a daydream; she hadn't tuned it all out. She had heard it and recognized that it was meant for her. We stepped into the small, private chapel in the back, and I held her for a long time. "You're right, honey," I agreed. "That one was all for you. God couldn't have spoken more clearly to you if he'd come down in a cloud." After that, Taryn stopped fighting about leaving, and then it was August 10, and she was gone.

The school year came to a close and summer vacation was in full swing. Kayleigh was dating a guy who occupied a lot of her time, so most nights I spent either alone in my room, bingeing and making magazine collages, or sneaking out drinking late at night with both of them in random parking lots. My relationship with Kayleigh became a little shaky because her boyfriend and I were constantly competing for her time. Nothing was too dramatic, though; she made time for both of us.

I wanted to get out of Naples desperately. I was bingeing and purging as wildly as ever, but I just wanted a change of scenery. My cousin had come down for spring break and we had been talking more frequently over the past couple months. He lived outside of Cleveland, Ohio, and the change sounded like just what I needed. We both asked our parents, and to my surprise, they both agreed.

So, I got on a plane and headed to Ohio, with every intention of ceasing my bulimic behavior for a few weeks. I was so excited I could hardly stand it. Unfortunately, my plan didn't go quite as smoothly as I had hoped. During my stay, my aunt was very kind and planned lots of activities for the two of us, and we had a lot of fun together, but I felt like I was missing out on the whole reason I came to Ohio: my cousins.

The loneliness I thought I would leave behind in Florida was still a constant. The first few days I managed to control my bulimia, but I eventually lost it and would stay up all night on massive bingeing episodes. I slept in late and spent most of the time on the computer or downstairs alone. I felt guilty for being so antisocial, but I was too depressed to change my behavior.

And then, when I least expected it, I got the phone call. The faith-based program to which I had applied months ago was offering me a spot on August 10. It was so soon. I listened very politely and agreed with everything the woman said; I was completely at a loss for words. I had made a plan. I was supposed to graduate in December. I was still supposed to be on the waiting list. I would start college in January and then I would be free but now what? I couldn't say yes, but I couldn't say no. I screamed and cried to my mother later on the phone about how I couldn't go. It just wasn't right and it just wasn't fair.

I left Ohio and flew to Denver where my parents picked me up. I read the book provided by the rehab program on the plane, trying to decide what to do. A part of me just wanted to be normal again, but another part just didn't want to let go. The bulimia gave me something to be proud of and made me feel better about myself; my tiny body was physical proof of my control and success, and everyone who saw me knew it. It comforted me when I had no one else and soothed my raging anxiety. I couldn't let go yet—maybe just a few more pounds and I would stop.

I got off the plane and met my parents. We gave each other an awkward hug; it was so hard to know what to say to each other at this point. We sat down and they told me that the terror had to end. I had to accept the opening at the program, stop the eating disorder altogether, or move out. My father even had estimates for how much it would cost for me to live on my own. I was horrified.

I nodded in agreement to their plan, swallowing my anger and pride because I knew, as much as I didn't want to admit it, I couldn't be on my own yet. It wasn't financially possible unless I sacrificed my coveted college dream. I told them I knew I needed to go; maybe because deep down, I did know that I needed to go. I resented them for the ultimatum, though, wishing that they had approached it differently. Wishing they had another choice.

The resentment was obvious throughout the month in Colorado. I was like a girl possessed, and I was completely out of control. I would sneak out of the house to drive to the grocery store while my family was out hiking, buy $100 worth of groceries, and keep them under my bed. I did this at least three times a week. All of the money I had saved up from working so hard was gone by the end of that summer.

One night I was desperate for a binge but was out of food and couldn't get to the store. My whole family planned an outing to a karaoke bar at a local hotel that welcomed kids and families. I faked sick; lying on the couch feigning a headache, I watched them leave one by one with a smile. As soon as their car had driven away, I grabbed my purse and ran out the door to catch a bus into town.

The bus came quickly and I breathed a sigh of relief—this was going to be easier than I had thought. All I had to do was run in, get the food, and catch the next bus home. However, after a quick shopping spree to pick up a cake, ice cream, and sundae supplies, I found myself sitting at the bus station for half an hour. I was getting nervous—I had no idea how long the karaoke would take, and if my parents came home and I was gone, it would be difficult to explain my absence. Plus, I would miss out on my one chance to binge and purge. I asked the girl next to me if she knew when the next bus was coming.

"Well, they only come every hour after eight, so probably another half hour I would guess," she smiled, glancing at my melting ice cream. I panicked. My family would surely be home by then. I couldn't wait that long, but what other choice did I have? I glanced down the road up to the top of the hill where the condo sat, wondering how far it was. It was uphill pretty much the whole way but only about a mile or two, so I set off walking.

The first two-thirds of the walk were in darkness minus the headlights of passing cars. There was no real sidewalk so I had to walk on the edge of knee-length grass, scared to death that something or someone would jump out at me. As I was reaching the foot of the final hill, my grocery bag broke and all of the little bottles of sundae fixings spilled out. Like an animal, I greedily snatched up my purchases, glancing around to see if anyone had seen. I looked up to the top of the hill and saw the condo and began to run, holding the groceries to my chest. I ran and ran and finally I was home. I took a deep breath, amazed that I had made it home in time.

My parents would hide food all over the condo in a desperate attempt to keep me from eating it all. It made me so angry because it created another obstacle, stopping my bingeing. I was desperate and resorted to stealing food from my aunt's apartments, claiming to be using their computers. I would search the condo to find a precious box of cookies or a few candies. And whenever I found them, I would eat them.

Meanwhile, my mother discovered I was smoking. I tried to keep it as discrete as possible, only smoking if I knew I would have a chance to wash up afterward. I knew my mother was sensitive to the habit since one of her sisters has had multiple health problems as a result of smoking and still can't quit, but I never anticipated another invasion of my privacy.

I came home from a morning walk and went under my bed to get a book out from my backpack, which felt abnormally light. I opened it to find the one carton of cigarettes I had left gone and only an empty pocket in its place. I screamed into my pillow, furious. I was so sick of being searched and spied on and manipulated by my parents, and it was making me angry. I stormed out of my room and ran into my mother. She sternly told me that we needed to talk.

"THAT WAS MY PROPERTY!" I screamed. "HOW DARE YOU? I earned the money to pay for those cigarettes and they belong to ME! You can't just go taking other people's stuff!" I was so angry I could hardly stand it. This was the last straw. After all, it's not like I was snorting cocaine or shooting up heroin—I was smoking a cigarette. And if they would stop invading my privacy, maybe they would stop finding things they didn't want to see!

They went on about me being seventeen and still two months shy of being old enough to buy my own cigarettes. My mind began to wander around the "our house, our rules" part, and this time I wasn't trying to hide anything. I wanted revenge.

I left the room thinking of everything terrible that I could do. First, I waited until they were out of their bedroom and stole forty dollars out of my dad's wallet to cover the expense of the cigarettes. I tried to calm down, telling myself that everything was fair and even. But I needed more.

They left for the airport to pick up a family member and I ate everything I could find, wildly bingeing and crying and screaming all at the same time. I hated feeling like I had no privacy, and I desperately wanted a space of my own. I wanted them to feel the way they made me feel so many times over: violated, betrayed, and vulnerable.

I purged massively in their shower. I kept jamming a toothbrush down my throat until I was literally choking on my own bile and blood. And suddenly I felt relieved. I knew exactly what this would do to them and I smiled in pure spite. I took a shower and curled up in bed with a book waiting for them to get home.

A few hours later when they called me into their room, I walked in, geared up for a fight. But my parents were already defeated. Everything I had wanted them to feel in my anger they had felt forty times over, and the look of pain in their eyes was more than I could bear. I felt horrible and guilty, and I spent an hour quietly cleaning up the mess in the shower. I sent my mom an e-mail that night with a poem I wrote, hoping it would soften her. It did, and eventually she forgave me.

I only had a few days at home before it was time to go to the second rehab program. I solemnly packed my things, disappointed and unsure of my next move. I hated the idea of another center, especially one so centered on religion. Although I had always been raised to believe in God, my faith had been shaken by the past year's events. I couldn't understand why any god would put me and my family through this.

Fortunately, an amazing priest and family friend celebrated the final Mass before I left. He gave a wonderful homily that hit strangely close to home, highlighting hunger and food in a spiritual sense. I began to cry and then to sob as he finished; I knew it was some kind of sign that I was making the right choice. I ran out the back of the church, embarrassed because of my flowing tears, and I saw my mother follow me out. We sat together for the rest of the Mass, holding each other and crying. Suddenly everything was going to be okay.

I finished packing and set all of my bags next to the front door a few days later. I called Kayleigh and Jaime and said good-bye, making them promise to write. I spent all night on the phone with a friend from my first rehab program, crying and listening to her tell me how proud she was of me. I was weary and unsure if I would ever be able to change, but I was afraid to tell anyone—I was tired of disappointing people.

And the next day, I was on another plane.

CHAPTER THIRTEEN

Amazing Grace

August to October 2004

I stepped off the plane in the Tennessee airport and made my way to where I was supposed to be picked up. Looking around, my hopes began to fade as no one approached me and I saw nothing with the name of the treatment center on it. I called my mother on a pay phone sobbing, "Mom, there's no one here! Where are they? Did they forget about me?" She called the center and cleared up the mix-up, and within a half hour a tall, dark-haired girl came up to me. She was surprisingly young and strikingly pretty; I was relieved that she wasn't weird like I expected.

The landscape was beautiful and the drive flew by. We arrived at the big house; it was simple in design but still impressive for a non-profit organization. Inside was just as pleasing; the foyer was filled with comfy couches and the kitchen was clean and well stocked.

There was a library filled with books and a huge backyard, including a porch with chairs and umbrellas.

Girls wandered the house unsupervised and alone; they would come up to me and ask me questions. It was so different from what I remembered about the first rehab program. The same woman who had picked me up from the airport searched through my suitcase for contraband items, although the rules were much more relaxed than before. When I was shown to my room it was bright and cheery, and I was surprisingly pleased. My roommate was outgoing and sweet and seemed genuinely excited to show me the ropes. We ate dinner together and I looked around at all the other girls hoping I would fit in here.

I made a few more friends on the couch after meals. All girls with eating disorders were required to sit on the couch for an hour after meals until their therapist designated otherwise. We would whisper to each other about what other treatment centers we had been to and what kinds of problems we had been through. Occasionally, girls who were not required to sit would join us, but the girls who had eating disorders found a special bond with each other in our hour-long imprisonment.

Overall, the rules were significantly less strict than what I had experienced in the first program. We could select our own meals instead of just picking up a tray; the catch was since I had a history with an eating disorder, I had to show my plate to a staff member. It didn't matter what I chose out of the buffets as long as I had the designated amount of carbohydrates, vegetables, and so on. Also, we were not supervised constantly. We had more downtime, which we could spend in our rooms, sitting on the couch, or sometimes sitting outside. We had recreation time every day and could choose what type of exercise we wanted to do.

The majority of our time was centered on God and Jesus. We would go to Bible reading in the morning, watch a videotaped sermon, sing praise and worship songs for an hour, watch another sermon at night, and go to church three times a week. Even though it was a lot of talking about a God I wasn't sure I was ready to trust, it was comforting to see girls who had been through horrible ordeals—things that I thought only happened in terrible movies—weep with joy for their God. It inspired me, and I started to read a few extra Bible chapters and started underlining everything encouraging I could find. And I finally started to pray again.

As time went on I began to have moments of feeling God's presence in a way that was completely new. During praise and worship sessions, I would fall to my knees in tears because I felt like I could feel God in the room. I would write letters to my parents about my renewed faith and how good it felt to be close to God again. I felt safe for the first time in forever.

Even though this program was much more relaxed, I only purged once. I started to adjust to living without the bulimia. Instead of every activity being centered on food and eating disorders, I spent time doing Tae Bo videos with a former cocaine addict and playing cards with a pregnant girl two years younger than me. I watched Disney movies on the weekends with a girl who had been in the hospital seven times for anorexia and walked around the mall with a girl who had spent a significant amount of time in a state mental institution for a dissociative disorder. I saw the happiness in their eyes, and for the first time I let myself wonder if life actually was better without the bulimia. After all, these young girls had been through more than most people go through in a lifetime. They helped me remember what it was like to laugh, and I actually let myself toy with the idea of recovery in hopes of truly finding happiness.

Unfortunately, despite my developments spiritually, I didn't find happiness. Coming from a Catholic background, I felt like a bit of a stranger among the many born-again Christians. Although I enjoyed the company of most of the residents, I only found a few girls to whom I felt close enough to trust, and I didn't believe anything the staff told me. All they ever said was how much they loved me and to keep praying. I didn't understand how a person could truly love someone they didn't even know.

I was freezing and exhausted all of the time. I would get frustrated over the silliest things because I was so on edge. Even though I felt a new love from God, I didn't feel much love around me. I felt isolated and alone.

A week before my birthday I carefully listed all of the pros and cons of staying in the program. I felt like I should go home, and I had an overwhelming number of reasons why. My parents had decided to come up and celebrate my eighteenth birthday with me, so I made up my mind to talk to them about my dilemma then. I could only hope they would be supportive.

And they were. They listened carefully as I explained all of the reasons why I was unhappy. I knew they would have a hard time understanding, but they treated me with a respect that I had never seen before. I felt like an adult as they simply outlined their concerns and fears. I wasn't just a child anymore that they could order around; I was free to make my own decisions.

And maybe that is what made me agree to stay for a little while longer. We said good-bye and I cried as they left, wondering if I would really be waiting for Christmas to see them again. As I walked back inside the building I suddenly felt the wave of loneliness rush over me again. I sat in a daze as a staff member checked me back in; for the first time in my life, I desperately wanted to go home.

This time, it was different for me. I didn't shed a million tears like I did when Taryn left for Arizona. I didn't feel the need or the desire to write to her every day, like I did the first time. It just didn't seem necessary. I wrote to her a normal amount of times and looked forward to our preplanned calls, but I didn't feel that frantic pull for constant updates and progress reports.

Similar to the first time she went to treatment, I was just glad she would be in a safe environment. Yet unlike that first time, I had no expectations of what would come from this experience. I just hoped and prayed.

While I still occasionally called the staff to check on how Taryn was doing, I knew that this was it—that our daughter had been given one more chance. When she was in Arizona, I almost felt a responsibility to stay involved on some level. This time, I felt more at peace that we had done our part. We had done all that we could do, and now she would work through her problems as she was meant to, and grow from it.

Soon my spirits started to lift. It was a combination of my newfound sense of peace and of Taryn being once again in safe hands. The cloud of tension was lifted, and I enjoyed the release. Taryn was supposed to be in this program for a minimum of six months. I now felt secure enough to relax and work on getting my life back.

I could focus more energy on the other girls, and that was a good thing. Although they rarely voiced their fears, I think it was difficult for them to have their sister repeating the treatment experience. After all, everyone knew how the last one had turned out. That had been damaging for the whole family—we'd had high hopes for Taryn, and they had been smashed. It was a tough pill to swallow for anyone, but especially for kids, who couldn't possibly understand all the psychological twists and turns. It was hard enough for Steve and me to understand, and often, we didn't.

During our weekend phone calls, I asked Taryn a lot of questions about the program and how they spent their time. It appeared that the daily schedule included a lot of meditative, alone time for the girls to reflect on the questions of the day. It was very different from the first center, where their time was more regimented, and there were so many different kinds of therapy. It would be interesting to see if this approach would reach into Taryn's soul and help her find the strength to climb out of her dark hole.

It was also a different experience for us in that we were not really a part of the process at all. There were no weekly sessions with her and her therapist. There was no Family Week. This was really about Taryn trying to figure out why Taryn was in this particular mess. And this was appropriate for the point we were at in the process. Steve and I were ready to admit that we didn't have the answers—we didn't have the quick fix. This belonged to Taryn.

At the Nashville home, she was exposed to girls experiencing a wide variety of troubles, including drug and alcohol abuse, depression and suicidal tendencies, unplanned pregnancies, eating disorders, and more. If I wasn't so frantic for Taryn to heal herself, I would have been more concerned that she was being exposed to some horrifying stories of young women who had been living in hell on earth. The home opened their doors to girls in need, and my daughter was one of them. I still found that hard to believe, and if I hadn't been so desperate to see her recover, I probably would have had a problem with the idea that we needed this kind of help, and that we were basically accepting charity.

The center had large donors who would offer opportunities to the girls, like a weekend at someone's amazing lake house or a trip to an inspirational concert or speaking engagement. My daughter was one of "the girls"—one of the recipients of a philanthropist's generosity, and I couldn't have been happier. We couldn't have afforded to send her away a second time, and she was getting help—that's all that I cared about.

While I still had no real answer as to why this all had happened, I didn't need to have one. I only needed to accept that these were our journeys. And I was more than ready to acknowledge that maybe God was the remedy, or at least the path to the cure. After seeing pure evil in Taryn's eyes, and watching the destruction, and witnessing the lies, manipulation, and malevolent havoc that was wreaked by this eating disorder, I was ready to believe that this could be a basic battle between good and evil. And if this was so, our child, the pawn, was in the right place.

The whole family flew to Nashville to help her celebrate her eighteenth birthday. It was almost exactly six weeks since she'd left, and we were excited to spend some time with her. When we saw her, she seemed different somehow. There was a maturity about her, as she gave us the tour of what had been her home for the last month and a half.

We were impressed. The facilities were so much nicer than we had expected, with comfy, elegant furniture and lovely bedrooms, which each girl shared with one other resident. Taryn's room was large and sunny, and the main living room was exquisite. The kitchen was clean and the stainless steel sparkled. The grounds were manicured and beautifully landscaped. We saw Taryn's classroom and all the different gathering spots. Everyone we met, both the staff and residents, seemed nice and friendly. It was a major reassurance to know she was in such comfortable surroundings.

We went out for dinner, and while we were waiting for a table, Taryn noticed a bookstore next to the restaurant. "Have you gotten me a birthday present?" she asked. I nodded yes, but then asked her why. "Well, it's okay," she answered. "It's just that I really would like to get this certain kind of Bible." I just looked at her, knowing that this, in itself, was a huge change, and I said, "Let's run over and see if they have it."

Later that night, Steve and I lay in the dark, talking. "She just seems so much more mature to me," I said to him. "Me, too," he responded. "I wonder if it's real." And that was a precursor to what would be our relationship with Taryn for several years to follow. Would we ever believe the words coming out of her mouth? Would we ever trust her again?

"I hope it's real," I whispered. "I hope they are getting through to her." We discussed the Bible purchase and her excitement at getting the Praise and Worship CD (the only kind of CD allowed at the home) from Taylor. I remembered when she'd sent us her birthday wish list, she'd added a postscript saying, *"FYI— I didn't mean for this note to be so selfish"* (for sending us her wish list). "Maybe she is growing up," I contemplated.

The next day, we explored Nashville from one end to the other. It was fun to have the family together enjoying a beautiful day. We came home for cake and more presents and sat outside to chat. The convivial atmosphere was broken with the six words we'd come to fear from Taryn. "I need to talk to you."

Uh-oh. Here we go. What could this be about? Steve and I sat in our chairs, purposefully not looking at each other. Those words just couldn't mean good news. We'd spent a lovely weekend, reassured about the quality of Taryn's living quarters and the program itself and thrilled with the progress it at least appeared that she was making. Now it was time for the bomb.

"I don't think I want to stay for six months," Taryn carefully began. "I'm not sure I need to stay anymore at all. And I have given this a lot of thought, and it's not a snap decision." We were silent, just staring at her. Inside, my alarms were at full alert, reverberating loudly, almost drowning out her words. We listened to her list all the reasons why she thought it was a good idea to leave.

"I'm always cold because they keep the place so freezing, and I'm always tired because they don't let us get enough sleep," she started, and then continued her inventory. "I feel like no one trusts me and I can't trust the other girls; I feel like I have to be careful around everyone. I feel falsely loved because they constantly tell me they love me, but they don't even know me. I feel uncomfortable with the charismatic church services and I miss the Catholic Mass. It's so loud there, I always have a headache, and the schedule is tedious—there's no variety. I'm not getting anything out of the therapy. We're basically going through a book. I'm frustrated because they are making it difficult for me to get my schoolwork done, and I feel really miserable and alone."

Then she wove her way into why she should leave. "I feel like I have my life on hold and everything's waiting until I get out of here," she complained. "I'd like the ability to make some money before college, and I could get my high school stuff and college SATs and applications done so much easier and faster at home."

Then, playing the faith card, she said, "I just have a feeling that I'm supposed to be at home."

Well, she'd done her homework. She delivered her litany of reasons and protests calmly and maturely. Her letters had made occasional mention of some of the problems she'd listed, but then the next card would be positive, so we'd hoped it was just a normal adjustment period. Steve and I glanced at each other, recognizing the same look of anxiety and disappointment that we each felt inside. But we weren't going down without a fight.

Taryn, wisely and like the legal adult she now was, asked for our opinions. We were impressed that she wasn't throwing a tantrum or begging for us to break her out. She was asking for our advice, and we were ready to give it. We weren't stupid enough to think we weren't being manipulated. Taryn was a very smart girl and knew exactly what buttons she needed to avoid and which ones to push. She also knew that at eighteen, she didn't need our permission to leave.

So we composed ourselves and started in on why we felt she should stay. We didn't mention because we thought we would need our own therapy if she came home early, or that we might explode with frustration at another failed recovery attempt. We kept it centered on her. We addressed all of her concerns, and then emphatically said we felt it was important to stay in a safe place— that it takes time to get over an addiction, and even if she felt she was doing well, it could all be for nothing if she left too soon. We told her the staff had warned her, and us, that the first two months were the hardest, and the urge to leave was the greatest. We reminded her that no one said this would be easy, but the goal was so worth the hard work.

The biggest gun in our arsenal was that she had signed a commitment paper before entering. She had promised that if they expended the time, money, and energy to give her this opportunity, she would give the program at least six months of her life. I felt it was a matter of honor and character to fulfill this commitment.

Taryn agreed that was one thing that bothered her, too. She also admitted that she felt closer to God and enjoyed the focus on learning about God. We jumped on that, trying to get her to see the positive aspects. Good Lord, she had to stay, we had to make her see that. In the end, we pulled out a little guilt, telling her our family couldn't handle another cycle of hope followed by despair. She owed it to herself to take the chance and try to make it work.

In the end, Taryn agreed to try. The commitment thing did nag at her, and she told us she did want to recover, so she'd try to get past all the things that annoyed her. When we dropped her off back at the home before our flight, it was tough to say good-bye. We hugged her and gave her as much encouragement as we could. We told her we loved her and looked forward to her visit at Christmas. I cried as we left her, knowing she was having such mixed feelings, and I prayed that she would stay strong in her decision to remain in treatment. I knew it was where she needed to be.

CHAPTER FOURTEEN

The Teacup

October to December 2004

We returned from our visit in Nashville feeling renewed and almost at peace. We were pleased with the improvement we'd seen in Taryn. She looked good, she seemed to be making progress, and our appraisal was bolstered by the knowledge that this was not the usual treatment facility. This was not a place that treated a patient with different sorts of therapies and lots of doctors. This was more about the patient treating herself through introspection—by digging deep and examining why she did the things she did. The counseling was to develop self-awareness and promote self-healing. That was why it was so important that it was the young woman who wanted to change her life, and not her family, spouse, or friends.

It had to be her. That one detail produced a small negative voice that nagged in the back of my mind. As content as I was, overall, with the status quo, there was that little question of our conversation—Taryn's doubt about whether this was working for her. I told myself that we had reasoned it out with her, and that she knew she had to see this through.

And yet, I couldn't escape the feeling that some of her arguments were thinly veiled manipulation. It was something we recognized now after a couple of years of practice. The whole missing the Catholic Mass thing—something she knew I'd like to think was true. And how about the "I have a feeling I'm supposed to be home" thing? Like that wasn't playing on my belief that everything is meant to be.

If she was still playing these games, would she really let go and allow other people to pull her strings for the next four and a half months? I made myself believe she would. Each time I received a letter or spoke to her on the phone, I tried to read or listen between the lines. I hung on every positive thing she would say, telling myself, "See, she's doing fine." And even though I still found I had to fight to ignore that annoying little voice, I went on with life, choosing to believe that it would all work out for my struggling daughter.

As I was busy answering all the curious questions about how Taryn was doing and where she was, I was getting other questions . . . from parents of kids with eating disorders. My phone number was listed in the paper under our adolescent eating disorder support group, and calls were coming in. Unfortunately, a few months after the group was started, the young facilitator, Betsy, began to have conflicts with the time. It became difficult to depend on her participation, and it was impossible to keep a group going under the circumstances.

When the summer came, it fell apart, as everyone was going in different directions, but we all talked about starting it up again in the fall. Even though Taryn wasn't in town, I was getting quite a few phone calls, so I tried to contact Betsy to see if we could get the group going again. After several days of no response, I called Betsy's mom, an acquaintance of mine. As soon as I broached the subject of Betsy and the group, I sensed uneasiness over the line. Finally the truth came out.

"It's just not going to work anymore," she admitted. "It was getting to her, bringing up old feelings from her past. She really wants to help these girls, but it's too hard on her, and I'm afraid it's not healthy for her to continue with the group." I paused, giving myself a moment to recover. We made a little more small talk and then said our good-byes.

Then I sat there for a few minutes, letting the news sink in. Betsy, the beautiful, upbeat, whirlwind of positive energy was still not past her eating disorder, which had been over for several years. Just being around the struggling girls had triggered a response in her so acute that she had to sever her ties to the group. God, how long was this going to remain with Taryn? Even if she did get over it, would a magazine article dredge it all back up? Would a casual conversation with a stranger make her get the urge? Would it ever be completely gone?

It wasn't long after this when I got the phone call from Taryn. She wanted to come home.

After my parents left, I continued with the program. Despite how hard I tried to look at the bright side and be cheerful, I was miserable. I was extremely frustrated. I had admitted to my therapist that I had purged during my first few weeks in the program, and I felt like I was being punished for it. All of my friends with whom I had spent hours on the couch had been "taken off" and were free to do whatever they wanted after meals. I was still stuck sitting on the couch in the freezing living room. I tried to bring a blanket and would curl up in it, but soon I was reprimanded because apparently blankets weren't allowed "on the couch." I wondered why this would encourage honesty—I never admitted anything to her again for fear that I would be stuck on the couch even longer.

I also had a very strange feeling that I was supposed to leave. Maybe it was nothing more than my homesickness and hatred of my surroundings, but I felt like I was being drawn to go home. My therapist wasn't as resistant as I thought, saying that if I wanted to leave, all I had to do was talk to the director. The fact that she didn't seem to care that I felt so bad was concerning; if she loved me so much why wasn't she trying to convince me to stay?

I sat in front of the director a few hours later, trying to be strong and explain why I wanted to go home. I explained to her everything, including my "feeling." I said maybe Jesus knew there was another girl out there who needed this spot more than me.

"Taryn, you were picked to come here for a reason. The staff prays so hard whenever a spot opens up. You were selected to come here because Jesus wanted you here. The devil is putting those thoughts in your head," she explained. I had grown very spiritual while I was away, but I still cringed when I was told that Satan was putting thoughts in my head. Even if no one else did, I trusted myself and my instincts.

My mother called and pleaded with me over the phone. She cried as she described how she had scrubbed my bathroom for hours to get the smell out. I was confident that I could control the bulimia at home; I told her not to worry and that everything was going to be different now. Eventually she gave up, telling me that it was my decision and as long as I was willing to pay for the flight, I could come home.

The few girls that I had grown close to during my short stay were, of course, hard to say good-bye to. I knew we would never be able to talk again because of policies the facility had, so I made myself as emotionally numb as possible; I wouldn't have had the strength to leave otherwise. I packed my bags and left, giving my friends hugs and holding back my tears, knowing in my heart I was making the best choice I could.

Instead of wild bingeing and purging like my last trip home from rehab, I spent the flight making nervous lists about my impending future. I sat in my seat on the airplane, drinking cran-apple juice with shaky hands, wondering how my disappointed parents would act when I arrived. Despite my uneasiness, I felt so much better on the airplane; no more guilt and a little bit of happiness. As I watched the countryside below me, I knew I had made the right choice. Another girl would be arriving in a few days, one who really wanted the services offered.

My parents were surprisingly calm and treated me like an adult. I nodded as they explained how I could live at home, but my eating disorder couldn't. If I was to continue, there could be no evidence of it anywhere. I was doing well and had no plans to start up again, so I figured that would be easy. I told them about my plans to get a job and finish up my high school online courses; I would apply to the University of Florida again and hopefully start school over the summer. They agreed and even gave me some suggestions on where to apply for a good full-time job.

Meanwhile, I called Kayleigh and my social life was in full swing again. She was partying more often, and since I just wanted to fit back in, I started dating lots of different guys and drinking a lot more. Kayleigh was dating the same guy, who seemed to have a problem with me, so we were still competing for her time. We saw each other often—parties at night, sneaking out, and smoking marijuana all the time. Even though I had become much more spiritual, having friends seemed more important than religion. My initial guilt soon dissipated; I was having so much fun that it was hard to regret my choices. Soon all of my nights were spent drunk or stoned in the backseat of a car—floating in some cosmic oblivion free of all my problems. Despite my behavior, I still tried to attend church regularly and managed to maintain a sense of spirituality.

Unfortunately, my eating disorder did come back. It was okay for about three weeks, and then I started gaining weight. I freaked-out and purged, and it was a hundred times easier than I remembered. Before I knew it, I was back into the swing of being bulimic and was bingeing and purging all the time again. This time, however, I kept it completely hidden from my family. If I could help it, I would purge somewhere else. I would drive out of my way to get to my favorite purge spots, the number one being the public library. The building had a handicapped bathroom that was its own private room instead of a stall, complete with sink and mirror and totally separate from the regular bathroom. No one could hear me or see me purging. If I had to purge at home, I always used plastic bags in my room. No smell, no mess, and no hassle.

Since Kayleigh was doing it, I also started smoking pot all of the time. I would get high two, three, four times a day—keeping me in a continuous haze. I could function without raising suspicions, but I could still feel the effect of the drugs. I loved the feeling—so thoughtful and deep. Anything and everything was taken in very slowly and analyzed to the finest degree; I discovered the meaning of life over and over every day. Kayleigh and I would sit on the beach at all hours of the night pondering random thoughts and just laughing at ourselves.

My life shifted back to being completely centered on food. The marijuana made me hungry and I binged and purged often. I would sit and imagine what I wanted to eat—fast food, cake, ice cream, pancakes—until I could hardly stand it anymore, and I would dash to my car and fill myself up past the brim—and then let it overflow into the toilet. I thought I was living the perfect lifestyle—I was thin and constantly on some kind of high.

I still don't know how much my parents knew. Even though I was already good at lying and hiding my tracks, I became even better. I always told them exactly what time I would be home and followed through. And I told them a place that I was going (even though usually I went somewhere else) and also made sure that my story would check out. I briefed all of my friends I was going out with as soon as we met up and made sure that everyone was telling their parents the same story. I always answered my cell phone and learned how to use hand sanitizer and Altoids to fake sober like a champ.

Then the bomb dropped and instantly my life charged. One night I went to Kayleigh's house to pick up something and she told me outright that she couldn't see me for a few days. I couldn't understand why, and when I questioned her hostility, she said she thought that I was only friends with her because of the marijuana. To this day I don't understand how a girl who, I would have given my life for could have thought that.

I began to sort of stalk her. I drove by her work and house several times a day, looking for her car, wondering what she was doing. Did she miss me? Should I talk to her? What will she say? Is she still mad? Have I served my sentence yet? Would she accept an apology? We had spent so much time together that when she disappeared I felt a huge void; our brief exchange haunted me. I lasted about four days until I finally broke down and knocked on her door. She slowly pulled it open, her eyes brimming with anger and hate. This was a side of Kayleigh I had never seen before, and I felt like a puppy that had just been kicked for no reason: scared, alone, and confused about what I had done to deserve this.

She started throwing harsh words at me and I got defensive because I didn't know how else to react. We fought violently and dramatically, screaming hateful things at each other. I went home that night sobbing and screaming and broken. I felt like someone had ripped out my heart and was tearing it apart in front of me; the pain was immense and on the verge of unbearable. My mother sat with me on my bed, scratching my arm, trying to make me calm down. My heart just ached and ached, and it was a few days before I could even function again. And I was always missing her.

I did eventually move on, and despite my dramatic social life, I was still diligently looking for a full-time job. One of my parents' suggestions was to apply at a certain exclusive golf club; my dad was friends with the head pro. I was a little hesitant because I am a terrible golfer and have never liked the sport, so I decided to apply to a few restaurants first since I was more familiar with the territory. Even though the season was about to start, no one at any of the restaurants where I wanted to work was really interested in hiring me. Disappointed, I called the golf club as a last resort and to my surprise was set up with an interview.

The club was unbelievably expensive to join and extremely private; the entrance didn't even have a sign. Once I found the place, I was buzzed in and immediately fell in love. The entrance drive was gorgeous, both sides of the street decorated with huge green trees. The club itself was equally as amazing, modeled after the old Florida style. I couldn't believe a place like this existed.

The head of the food and beverage department interviewed me, saying there was a job opening at the ninth hole snack bar. I would be paid a great hourly wage plus overtime and would be in charge of helping members, keeping the place clean, and inventory once a month. I jumped at the opportunity; I couldn't believe how lucky I was to not have gotten those other jobs.

I showed up in the white oxford shirt they provided, complete with the golf club's logo embroidered on it, and black dress pants. Karen, the head waitress, showed me around and helped me find everything during those first few days. Although she seemed a little tough at first, she really grew on me and I looked up to her.

The rest of the staff seemed fun as well. Sierra was another waitress who was a few years older than me, but we got along extremely well. I would check the schedule and look forward to every day we got to work together because we would be laughing the entire shift. Mark was a cook who worked in the kitchen and he was my first real friend. We would sneak out back and smoke cigarettes since we were the only two employees who smoked besides the caddies. On slow days, he would come over and hang out with me in the snack bar and teach me how to play Texas Hold 'Em, betting cigarettes and pennies.

My boss seemed a little anal, but nice. My dad's friend, the head pro, was funny and sweet, and the golf staff consisted of mostly cute guys in their twenties. The job was better than anything I could have ever dreamed; I made good money, the staff was fun, and the environment was beautiful. And it didn't hurt that I got to ride around in a golf cart a couple of times a day.

The members were also amazing. I didn't know what to expect in the beginning, but I still worked hard memorizing names, faces, and orders. Most of them were friendly and sweet, joking with me because I was new the first few times they visited my snack bar. I tried hard to make sure the water coolers were full and the fruit cooler always had a lot of variety. And most of them seemed to like me, so it worked out well.

During my first few days on the job, I tried desperately not to eat anything at work. Unfortunately, the kitchen staff cooked hot lunch for all of the employees every day, and the tantalizing smells always made their way to my little corner in the snack shop. I only made it about a week before I finally broke down and ate two helpings of the fantastic lasagna, my mouth watering at the scent of extra garlic bread. I turned on the merchandise that I was supposed to sell. Candy bars, regular sodas, hot dogs, and anything I could find in my small nook was suddenly prey to my monstrous appetite. I left my station and purged in a bathroom that was rarely used, my supervisor calling me on the walkie-talkie the whole time, wondering why SHE was helping MY customers. I later swallowed the lump in my throat as I shamefully received her reprimand.

And I did try hard not to do it again. I started having to buy candy bars and stuff them in my purse so I could replace all of the ones I stole. I kept a piece of paper in a cabinet where I would mark every candy bar I ate, ashamed and guilty. I knew how much trouble I would get into if someone found out, but I couldn't stop. A part of me hated it but another part made me crave it even more. I was completely out of control.

Yet, I still enjoyed it. I felt so rebellious and dark: I was getting into trouble and my parents had yet to notice a thing. Despite the "deal" we made when I first came home, I figured as long as I was just doing "normal teenage stuff," I wouldn't be kicked out. The heart of the deal was the part about bulimia. I was still exceptionally careful, taking steps to plan the perfect crime over and over each day. And it usually worked; I would sneak out to hang with friends and sneak back inside, no one suspecting a thing. But there was something missing in my life. Even though I was living like a rock star, I was getting sick of not giving a damn. I needed to care about something . . . or someone.

And then I met Sean. He was a member of the golf staff and worked outside, parking cars and helping members. I actually hated him at first. He was so overwhelmingly nice; it was a little too much for me to handle. I tried to avoid him, but since we worked together, it wasn't easy. He would come in and visit me during lunch—just to say hi. Eventually we started talking more and more, and I started to like being around him. He was so funny and seemed genuine.

The first time we went out together was a blur. I never thought our friendship would last, and I certainly didn't think it would develop into anything more. Sean was just not my type. He didn't drink or smoke, and I felt like he was my exact opposite. We were nothing more than friends seeing movies and going out to dinner— it was fine for a while.

There was something very attractive about him that I just couldn't seem to pinpoint, however. He was very handsome, but also eleven years older than me. Although age never stopped me before, I was afraid that anything romantic would ruin our friendship. I knew I could really care about him, but I was afraid; I hadn't been close to anyone since Kayleigh. Nevertheless, I slowly started to have a little crush.

We started hanging out more and more. We would go out to dinner all the time and take long walks afterward just talking about nothing really, but it was nice to have someone to talk to. We would hug and even sometimes stand right up next to each other with our lips barely touching, but we never kissed. It was the most amazing experience of my life; the anticipation was incredible. I had never felt like this before . . . this strange, warm feeling that I hated at first.

My mother was very curious about my new friend, but I wasn't sure how she would react to the age difference. Ever since my friendship with Kayleigh had ended, I had stopped hanging out with people my own age. Since I wasn't going to high school, it was hard to find a lot of teenagers with whom I could be friends. I decided to bring Sean over to meet my family before I told my mom the truth. The night I introduced Sean went well; he seemed to pass the test. I smiled as my family laughed at all his jokes, and Taylor whispered to me later how cute he was. It calmed my nerves as I faced my mother.

She seemed to have a few concerns, but surprisingly, she didn't forbid me from seeing him. I told her we were just friends, which was the truth; we still hadn't even kissed. I could tell she didn't believe me, but I didn't press the issue. Whether she wanted to believe we were friends or not, she was still allowing him to come over and spend time with me. It was funny how misplaced her suspicions were since this was the most innocent relationship of my life.

Sean and I officially started start dating in late December and took a trip to Disney World about a month later. And there, in the Epcot parking lot, we finally kissed for the first time. It was glorious. I had been waiting for this moment for months, and it was perfect. I had never had so much build up for anything in my life, and I was in love with the feeling.

We started kissing more and seeing each other almost every night. I slowly began to come out of my madness. I quit smoking—both marijuana and cigarettes—and quit drinking minus a few beers here and there. I began to actually sleep somewhat normally, and I wasn't swinging wildly from one emotion to the next. I actually even began to like myself a little bit . . . Sean made me feel worthwhile and special—things I hadn't felt in a long, long time.

My self-esteem slowly started to improve. I became stronger with the help of positive influences, including my therapist, Kit. The medicines were starting to work, and she was a good listener; sometimes it was nice to have someone objective to talk to. I don't remember very many "breakthroughs" or "big discoveries," but what I remember is how she never judged me, an unusual trait, even among therapists. So I told her everything. It was nice to get it all off my chest.

My eating disorder was still a big part of my life, but not as strong as it used to be. With my self-confidence starting to grow, I didn't need it as much as I used to. Sean made me feel good, separate from the bulimia; my family was smiling again, and every day was looking a little brighter for ME, not me and my entourage of issues. Mentally, I was ready to let go; I just had to find a way to stop the addiction.

Certainly I wasn't completely surprised by the news that only two short weeks after our visit, Taryn wanted out of treatment. I was starting to learn that the little nagging voice was rarely wrong. "Taryn, what about everything we talked about?" I asked her. "Your commitment, your recovery."

"Mom," she answered, "I just don't need this. I can do this on my own, and I'm sick of being frozen, tired, and miserable. I'm ready to start the rest of my life."

I begged her to just give it some more time, to think about it a little more. Her therapist, Marisa, called to tell me that Taryn had activated their exit process by telling her she no longer wanted to stay there. I had a very long, impassioned discussion with her, asking her advice, trying to form an alliance to talk Taryn into staying.

There were several steps Taryn had to complete to leave the facility. She had already spoken to her therapist, which was step one, and she would need to talk to the director. If at that time her mind was still made up, she would have to leave within twenty-four hours. I was frantic. After all we'd been through, I was finally feeling like life was on the right track. I sensed that Taryn needed time almost more than anything else, and in Nashville, her time would pass in a controlled, safe environment. After six months, she could truly be over the worst of it, but after two months? I could envision her falling right back into the darkness.

I felt like it was a race against time. I spoke to any staff person I could reach, asking them to talk to Taryn and try to help her understand. It had taken months of waiting, piles of paperwork, countless questionnaires and medical exams to get Taryn where she was, and now, after only two months, she wanted to give it up. And she was eighteen. There was nothing I could do.

I spoke to her a couple more times, pleading with her to reconsider, but not going so far as to threaten her or order her to stay. I recounted the obvious reasons to remain, and she came back with her own legitimate-sounding reasons to go. I told her she would have to pay for the flight home, since it was against our wishes. No argument from her. "I understand," she said. And then, the director was on the phone. "Mrs. Benson, I'm afraid Taryn has made up her mind to leave our program." Here were the words I was dreading. "It is her decision, and this means that she will have to leave right away."

Needless to say, we weren't happy that she opted not to stay the six months. And we were very afraid. As I quickly made plane reservations for Taryn's trip home, Steve and I sat down for what seemed like the millionth time to map out our newest game plan. We might not have been able to control Taryn's decisions, but we could control our own lives, and we damn well were going to do that.

After waiting for months for our daughter to be accepted into the Nashville program, and then settling into a skeptical but hopeful calm while she was there, we were now a little ticked off and a lot disappointed that she was on her way home. We sat down with her the minute she walked in the door.

Once again, we laid out our ground rules. We would not live the way we had been living. And we would no longer expose the other girls to the chaos. We expected that she would continue her therapy, but she was to be in charge of making sure she made her own appointments. If she chose to return to her eating disorder, we did not want to see one bit of evidence that it even existed.

"When you left in August, I scrubbed every inch of your bathroom, the walls, every tile," I bluntly reminded her. "I washed the shower curtain, the rug, and anything I could find that might have that awful smell on it. For weeks, I'd walk by there and still smell that faint, putrid mix of vomit and cover-up perfume." I knew this was brutally frank, but I needed her to appreciate my position. "I'd keep going back, finding something else to clean until finally, it smelled clean. I don't ever want that in my house again." Taryn looked at me and nodded.

"We're done trying to micromanage your recovery," I told her. "You're old enough now to realize it's your life, and you're responsible for what happens to you." Then we brought up the subject of trust. Once again, by abandoning her commitment and leaving the program, our trust in her was broken.

We reminded her of the story we'd recounted many times over the years—the "Teacup" story. The tale was about a teacup that was broken and glued back together. Although they were hard to see, the cracks were still there, and they were a weakness in the cup. It was possible to use the cup again, but it was never quite the same as before the break. "We've lived with a lot of lies," I said seriously. "We are asking you for honesty in all things now, Taryn. One lie will set us back light-years."

After telling her she was welcome to live at home, finish high school, work, save money, get ready for college, whatever, we informed her she would have to abide by our house rules, including curfew. "If you can't honor our wishes, you will have to live elsewhere," Steve warned, knowing we would now live in fear that we might have to make good on this one day.

This was the beginning of a change in our lives. Everything was on the table. We were through having the eating disorder dictate our lives to us. We had sent her to two facilities and spent thousands on therapy, doctors, and medications. We had lived with her as we watched her bones protrude. We had personally witnessed the sickening, terrible cycle of bingeing and purging. We lived through her countless depressions, mood swings, and sleepless nights perhaps caused by the Pandora's Box of medications she'd been given. And we had learned way more than we ever wanted to know about noticing a fresh slice on our child and recognizing that it was self-inflicted.

We also knew the pain of being separated from our daughter and placing her care in someone else's hands—of missing her and agonizing over whether or not we'd done the right thing. And now she had chosen to come home against our wishes. We were done.

Taryn knew there would be no parade to welcome her home—that we believed with all our hearts that she would have a better chance at achieving everything she wanted if she had stayed in Nashville, and that coming home was a mistake. I couldn't be sure, but I wondered if maybe she really did think that she had absorbed enough from the program to go it on her own. Or was it just another ploy to descend back down the rabbit hole? I didn't for a second imagine that the eating disorder was gone. The best I was hoping for was that maybe she was ready to actually try to recover on her own.

Taryn was smart enough to know on what side her bread was buttered. Fortunately, she did have goals: she wanted to finish high school and get into the University of Florida. If that meant playing it our way, she would. It appeared that she respected our approach; that we hadn't fought her tooth and nail over leaving the treatment center, and that we were treating her like an adult. All we needed now was trust.

That was going to be hard, if not impossible, to attain. It didn't take Taryn long to find a good-paying job at a prestigious golf club, running the ninth hole snack shop. Since she was finishing her last few high school requirements online, she could work a regular day job. Although she was still working with food, there was a lot more accountability, no cash, and less opportunity to get into trouble. At least that was what I thought. I had no confidence that all was well in her world, however.

As Taryn settled into her routine, I had to give her credit that she was either getting her act together or doing a great job of hiding the evidence. There was no sign of her eating disorder in our home. My maternal instincts were telling me everything wasn't picture-perfect, but she was following our orders and not bringing it home. I didn't notice food missing, and she didn't make a beeline to the bathroom after meals. She called to tell us what she was doing, and she was home on time. Even so, Steve and I questioned everything; if not to her, to each other. "Do you think that's where she really is?" he'd ask. "I wonder if she's purging on the job," I'd say. We just could not believe a word she said.

We realized we just couldn't trust her anymore, no matter how much truth she might throw at us. We had been through too much manipulation for too long, and this was the legacy. Even if we wanted to believe her, we simply couldn't. Our doubting minds wouldn't let us. And it created a perfect catch-22. She would try to tell us the truth. We wouldn't believe her. She would want us to trust her, so she'd lie about something stupid so she wouldn't get in trouble. We'd find out, and bingo—more ammunition to not trust her. And then we'd doubt most of what she'd already told us. This was clearly going to be a stumbling block for a long time.

As her social life picked up, we were once again in the old quandary. We wanted her to have normal experiences with friends, but we were afraid of the type of fun she might find. She gave us no concrete proof that she was engaging in any dangerous behavior, and we never suspected that she ever left after we'd go to sleep. She had learned to be not only a consummate liar but an accomplished escape artist as well.

When Taryn had her falling out with her longtime friend Kayleigh, I felt so bad for her, and we sat together, rehashing the story as she tried to figure out why the friendship had gone so unexpectedly wrong. I remember being so angry with Kayleigh. Her seemingly arbitrary actions trampled all over Taryn's barely budding self-esteem, and I feared the possible repercussions. I had no clue that Taryn was probably better off without her negative influences. I only knew that during this fragile time of reconstruction, the last thing my daughter needed was her so-called best friend to bail out on her. The mother lion in me was still alive.

Soon, however, her troubles with Kayleigh were put on a back burner by a new distraction. I began picking up on increasing references to a friend of hers from work, Sean. I also picked up on vibes that let me know I wouldn't approve of everything about Sean. After meeting him, we had a prolonged Q & A session, she gave up the problematic detail—he was eleven years older than Taryn.

This was an entirely different can of worms. Although she insisted they were just friends, my trusty intuition was singing a different song. It may have started as just friends, but it was heading somewhere else, and fast. She told me I would love him. "He doesn't smoke, or drink, or have sex. I can't believe he's my friend," she laughed. And when she brought him around, we could see why she liked him. He was handsome, funny, and very young for his age.

More importantly, I could see a positive change in Taryn. Sean made her feel good about herself. She was having fun, laughing, enjoying herself. I wasn't happy about the age difference, but their relationship didn't seem to be a bad thing. In fact, it appeared to be the opposite. I hoped they'd remain "just friends," but the writing was slowly starting to show up on the wall. And since she was eighteen, I wasn't going to have a lot of influence in that department.

I wish I could say I followed through with total consistency on our resolution to give Taryn ownership of her recovery. I still kept an eye on her calendar, asking when her next appointment with Kit would be, or if she wanted me to call Dr. Paul's office for her. But I was much better, and I was especially improving in realizing that whatever struggles Taryn had, this was part of the challenge that she needed to face alone.

We began to forge a coexistence based on respect, if not trust.

CHAPTER FIFTEEN

The First Light

December 2004 to Present

It was sometime after the holidays when I found myself taking inventory. Was it really almost two years since our nightmare with Taryn had begun? On one hand, it was all kind of a blur, and suddenly our daughter was grown up. On the other hand, it was two of the longest years of my life. It felt like we had been battling this all-consuming eating disorder forever. I was now almost a local expert on the subject, and people called for advice, or just to talk to a parent who understood. It was still rather amazing to me that this was now a part of my life.

Things at home had settled into a rhythm, with more good days than bad ones. In our quest for honesty, I had started asking Taryn the occasional question of how things were going. The difference now was she didn't seem to mind my asking, at least most of the time. Sometimes, she would clam up as if to tell me to mind my own business.

When she was feeling open, she would tell me last week had been a bad week, but since then she'd been doing great. Or that she'd had a tough time fighting the urge at work one day but felt good that she'd resisted. We actually began to have sporadic dialogues once in a while about the bulimia. And they were strangely adult-type discussions. Even so, I could never be sure if what she was telling me was true or just another myth she was fabricating to keep us in the dark.

Of course, I wanted to hear that she was over it; that somehow, she no longer needed her eating disorder, and it was mysteriously a thing of the past. That wasn't the way it worked, though. I knew what the party line was—it can take five years from the time you decide to recover before the battle is won, and like alcoholism, it often stays under the surface, something to be dealt with one day at a time. The question was, had Taryn decided to recover? Was she now on the long road to restore her health, or was it all a facade?

Because of our lack of trust, there was no real way to know for sure. On the surface, it looked like she was trying to get her life back. When people would ask me how she was doing, I would answer that I thought she was doing pretty well. The operative word was "thought." I couldn't know. But she laughed more, attended family dinners without it being an issue, and wasn't walking around like she was cursed. And although I no longer was overcome with the need to snoop, the few times I was legitimately looking for something unrelated in her room, I found no grisly discoveries in the closet or under the bed. In my book, all of this called for a little optimism.

Taryn finished high school online without fanfare. There was no real celebration because it was basically a final click of the computer mouse. I still held out hope that maybe she would attend her graduation. She'd been robbed of so many of high school's rites of passage, and I didn't want her to miss one more, especially such a major one.

As for college, we asked her to stay in Florida for the first year, so we could at least monitor her health more often than if she was out of state. With two inpatient stays and countless disruptions, she had still finished 26th in her class of 548, with a 5.0 GPA. We felt it was a shame, albeit a necessary one, to restrict her choices, but it turned out University of Florida was her first choice whether she was limited or not. Almost a year after her first invitation to UF arrived, her second acceptance letter was delivered, and we were thrilled.

With her immediate future secured, Taryn's days were filled mostly with work, and increasingly with her good "friend," Sean. Sure enough, she eventually confessed that things had progressed to more than a friendship. While we weren't thrilled with the age difference, we could see Sean really cared for Taryn and vice versa. If what Taryn was informing us was true, sex was not a motivation on his part, and my gut was telling me the same thing.

The relationship was clearly having a positive effect on our daughter. We wondered how it would all work out when Taryn left for school in the summer, but meanwhile, the smallest seed of hope grew as less time was spent worrying if she seemed better or worse that day.

Even as our day-to-day life improved, our concerns weren't over. There was the much older boyfriend, but there was also the pharmaceutical smorgasbord that Taryn was being prescribed. Since her stay at the first facility, she had been on an antidepressant, but since then, her medications had been switched several times, and a variety of antianxiety drugs had been introduced to the mix, including an antipsychotic. That freaked me out—an antipsychotic? And this begged a whole new set of questions.

Were the drugs necessary? How were they interacting with each other? How were they affecting her behavior, and what effect, if any, did they have on her bulimia? As a parent, there was definitely a part of me that wanted to see Taryn off all the meds, just to see if this had been a hormonal, coming-of-age thing, a medical condition, or even a chemical imbalance. Taryn still had insomnia, volatile mood swings, and periods of depression.

Throughout the eating disorder ordeal, Taryn, always innately curious and mentally ordered, needed to have a reason for why this happened to her. So many of her friends had gone down a similar path, only to discard the behaviors and move on to other activities. Why had she been held in the disorder's grasp?

Over the months, she would research on the computer and come to her sessions with Kit armed with potential medical reasons for her problems. At various times, Taryn was sure she had bipolar disorder, clinical depression, obsessive-compulsive disorder, borderline personality disorder, and generalized anxiety disorder. Sometimes Kit would agree that the diagnosis was possible, and sometimes she would disqualify it for one reason or another. Depending on what Taryn was experiencing, she would tweak her medication or add something different.

Being a bit conservative when it comes to pills and chemical solutions, I was very uneasy with many of the pharmacy fixes. I definitely wanted Taryn to be happy and to enjoy life, but I'd heard so many stories of teenage angst that I couldn't help but wonder if it was possible that, as Taryn matured, many of her issues might dissipate naturally. And could the various drugs she was taking contribute to or cause many of the adverse symptoms she was experiencing?

I found myself wishing she could wean herself off everything. But I could see she had anxiety, and I believed depression accounted for some of her difficulties, so I backed off and trusted her doctor.

Throughout this time, I felt periods of confirmation that truly we all have challenges that we are meant to fight our way through, and from which we need to learn. By accepting that this was not only true for me, but for Taryn as well, my journey was made bearable, and I knew that this knowledge would help me as the journey continued. It was dawning on me that the old cliché, "It is through the challenges that we grow" was pretty much on the mark.

Before I knew it, it was time for graduation. I tried one more time to persuade Taryn to walk with her class. "Honey, it's a once-in-a-lifetime thing," I begged. "You missed prom and so many other things that only happen in high school. Are you sure you want to take a chance on regretting missing this?" She was sure. She was no longer in high school mode and hadn't been for quite a while. She had spent the last eight months working full-time and had no interest in spending several hours in an indoor arena celebrating something she'd actually accomplished months earlier. "No party, Mom," she said. "Just a family dinner."

And so it was. We gave her several gifts, including Maria Shriver's book, *And One More Thing Before You Go,* on the transition from high school to college for a young woman. I loved her ten rules of wisdom and guidance on leaving your family and facing your new life in college.

We dropped Taryn off at the University of Florida for the summer session on our annual trek to Colorado. We helped her move in, dodging the sporadic raindrops as the afternoon thunderstorms rumbled around us. We met her roommate and relished our own college memories as kids poked their heads in to say hi, and new friendships were born in the hallways between trips to the car. We knew our farewells would be bittersweet, even more than most families experienced when they dropped their sons and daughters off to start their independence.

We knew her struggles weren't over, so there was that small sensation of liberation that our day-to-day lives would have less lies and a little less stress in them. We knew we'd have that worry whether she would keep up her therapy, stay on the recovery course (if she was indeed on it, since we couldn't know for sure), or, without us to look over her shoulder, relapse into darkness again. But we also knew we would miss her scathing sense of humor, wit, and the place she held in our family. No matter what happened, this chapter in our life was closing, as Taryn embarked on her own course. And I now understood that it was part of her journey, not mine.

I had shed a lot of tears the last couple of years over Taryn, and when I didn't break down sobbing before our departure, I figured it was because I was cried out. I could feel the tightening of my chest and a little welling in my eyes, but I somehow managed to keep my emotions under control as we kissed and hugged, and then she was busy trying to set up her room. It was time to go. Right before we left, she handed me a folded note that said "To Momma" with hearts on the outside. Once we were safely ensconced in our packed car and making our way out of Gainesville, I opened the note.

> Mom, Inspired by the book you gave me, I have made my own little list for you . . .
>
> (1) Remember I am growing up in a very different world than you did. The same rules do not apply.
> (2) If I call you in tears, I am looking for support, not advice.
> (3) Don't even think about using my room for some type of sick bird sanctuary.

[Taryn like to tease me about my pet finches].

(4) I'll probably never be an easy, perfect, or even
    predictable kid, but I'll turn out alright in the end.
(5) I love you. You are a wonderful friend and mentor, and I
    care about you very much. Thank you for everything.

Love, Taryn

And once again, she made me cry. Only this time, it was because I could see the light at the end of the tunnel.

My self-esteem continued to rise, and finally my raging bulimia slowly started to improve. Of course it didn't stop altogether, but I began going hours and then days and sometimes even a week without a single purge. I maintained my weight and exercised; from some standpoints it looked like I was suddenly healed. I didn't have to fast before I shopped for a new pair of jeans, and every now and then I actually liked what I saw in the mirror. I was confident about my future and things were looking up.

Kit and I had been trying different combinations of medicines since I had started seeing her, and it seemed like we were getting close to the right blend. My anxiety was quieter, depressive episodes less frequent, and my mood was generally stable. I started to feel confident in myself and happy with my life. There wasn't very much to complain about: I had a boyfriend who adored me, I had finished high school in the top of my class despite countless drawbacks, and my job was great.

I applied and was accepted to the University of Florida for the second year in a row. I also scored high enough on my SATs to qualify for a full scholarship. Everything was happening so fast, and my future was falling into place. My mother begged me to walk with my class at the graduation ceremony, but I had no interest. High school seemed so far behind me; besides, my memories of high school were horrible, and I didn't really want to revisit them. I told her if she needed some form of celebration, the only thing I would commit to was a family dinner.

My life was coming together nicely; my only complaint was that I didn't have very many friends since I had left high school behind. Even though I have never been a "girly girl," I missed that female companionship in my life. The wounds from Kayleigh were still fresh and painful, and I never felt like the issues surrounding our fallout had ever been addressed; but I tried to bury my pain by working or spending time with Sean.

One day in late February, my mother told me that Kayleigh had been in a near-fatal car accident. I reacted extremely emotionally and spent the next couple of months making efforts to show her I was thinking of her.

I called her parents once a week for updates during the rest of the time she was in the hospital. I sent both Kayleigh and her mother cards, and as soon as Kayleigh came home, I dropped off a colorful bag filled with several unique gifts that I handpicked because I knew they would make her smile. Despite all of my efforts, I still heard nothing from her; not one phone call or note. I kept thinking that she must simply not be feeling up to it, even though her parents said she was off crutches and gaining energy every day.

So one afternoon I got off work a few hours early and decided to stop by her house. She seemed excited to see me and she explained how she had been meaning to call but so much had been going on that it had slipped her mind. She thanked me profusely for the gifts and said that they meant more to her than any other gifts she had received.

We talked about her boyfriend and she told me that after the accident, while she was near death in the hospital, he had tried to convince the cops that she had been the one driving so he wouldn't get a DUI. In spite of this, they were back together. My stomach twisted; after all, she had dropped me for no real reason at all, but she took him back after he tried to blame her for the accident that nearly killed her. But I continued smiling with pure happiness, and we made dinner plans. I was thrilled. I told both my mother and Sean and both warned me to be careful.

A surprise to everyone, Kayleigh was true to her word and kept the dinner plans. I picked her up and we went to a restaurant and ate salad; she told me that she was a vegan now. We talked about astrology and religion and laughed like we used to. Everything seemed back to normal, and it felt like nothing had changed. She even called me her best friend again. I had never been happier. We parted ways that night promising to call each other the next day and maybe go to the beach or the mall.

But she never did call again. I tried to contact her, but she never answered her phone or responded to my messages. Within a few days she sent me an e-mail. "Please leave me alone," she wrote. "I thought I made it pretty clear that I can't be your friend right now." She had stabbed me again. I couldn't believe I had been this stupid. I e-mailed her back, begging her to explain to me what happened this time. I was so confused, and I only wanted to understand what I had done that was so wrong.

Although she never directly influenced my eating disorder, Kayleigh's second unexplained rejection shook me to the core. My self-esteem was significantly damaged, and it was difficult to deal with the emotions I felt. She had been a constant throughout my entire eating disorder nightmare, and eventually I realized losing her was for the best. I needed to break away from her manipulation, and in the end it helped me learn how to fully break away from my bulimia. Losing a close friend is a long and difficult process, and it takes many true friends to make up for the one who betrays you.

I had difficulty the first few months in college controlling my bulimia. Being on my own with no one babysitting my bathroom use was all too tempting. I had a roommate my first semester who was also very diet-conscious, so that made it much more difficult to forget about food. However, I was much more confident in myself than I had ever been before. I was more comfortable with myself, and I felt like I could stop bingeing and purging if only I could find a way to force myself to go a little while without it.

I got my wish when I was told I needed to have my wisdom teeth taken out. I spent a week and a half with a face swollen like a chipmunk and couldn't have purged even if I had wanted to. The ten days off broke the pattern, and I found it easier to use all of the tools I had learned to help me recover. By the time I was fully functional again, I was adjusting to life without bulimia, eating regular meals and keeping them down. I still slipped some days, but I was finally able to let go.

Sean and I eventually separated because of the distance. Our relationship helped me grow a lot as a person and, most importantly, gave me self-esteem. It was the first time someone besides my immediate family had ever really cared about me, and it made me realize that I was worthwhile. With the help of him and the other people around me, I grew to become confident in myself and my abilities.

I consider myself recovered now and haven't been in a steady binge-purge cycle for more than two years. I still make mistakes every now and then, but overall I am healthy. I try to eat as well as a college student can, and I make an effort to spend time exercising. And except for a few occasional bad moments, I am starting to see myself the way everyone else sees me; I'm learning how to take off the eating disorder glasses when I look in the mirror. I'm through the hardest part, and have reached the light at the edge of the dark tunnel.

EPILOGUE: PART 1

Off to Wherever

Probably the most common question I get when people learn I am a recovered bulimic is if I could go back in time, would I make different decisions? If I had the chance to start over, would I want to be "normal"? Would I change the past?

I always answer no. My eating disorder cost me so much—money, friends, valuable years of my life, and my parents' trust. It stripped me of my pride and self-esteem and left me a pile of bones, but I would never change my experience. It gave me something so powerful that I wouldn't trade it for anything. The past few years of my recovery have proved that I am strong—stronger than I ever thought I could be. And I am confident in who I am. I don't need anyone to make me feel good about myself, and the fact that I overcame a disease that kills 10 percent of its victims is amazing to me.

Writing this book was difficult because it brought up so many emotions that I would rather forget. I had to look through journals that I had written and see the disturbing images I had cut out of magazines or found on the Internet; I suddenly remembered how it felt to starve as I saw my careful logs of food intake. It made me cry and wonder how this girl could have ever existed. I felt so much pain for her, knowing that even though I have left her behind, she still exists in the souls of other victims.

I'm still not perfect. And I'm not trying to be anybody's poster girl for eating disorder recovery. I represent reality. This isn't a Pollyanna story where everything ends up perfect and everyone is happy . . . this is a long, slow attempt to sew up the hole I fell into. Or rather, jumped into.

And my stitches are not all neat and in perfect order. Recovering from an eating disorder is horribly difficult and takes endless time and patience. If I mess up I have to backtrack and figure out where I went wrong; sometimes I have to go all the way back to the beginning. But I start over again. I always start over again, and that is the important thing. The experts say true recovery usually consists of two steps forward, one step back. And slowly, eventually, you get to the point where the only direction you are going in is forward, with the hole all stitched up so that you won't fall in again.

As terrible as it began, the journey has been truly an amazing one. Although I didn't recover directly from the treatment centers, I learned so much about self-esteem, and the tools that I was given for recovery did help me—as soon as I was ready to use them. All of the girls that I met had powerful stories, and I learned so much from each and every one of them. I have been given opportunities to reach out and help other victims; a teacher I had in middle school invited me to speak to her eighth graders about bulimia. I discovered faith and realized its power.

And I have grown closer to my family than I ever thought possible. My sisters are my best friends—even though we are all at very different times in our lives. Taylor is a recent high school graduate and quickly growing into a funny and beautiful young woman. Little Halli, who has always been my baby sister, is suddenly not a baby anymore; she is smart and athletic, funny and mature. I admire so much in both of them and like to think that they learned a lot about themselves throughout this whole experience, too. My father, who often seemed to be in the distance during the eating disorder, is warm and happy again. The worry and fear is gone from his eyes and instead I see joy. I respect him so much—it takes a lot of confidence for a man to be able to sacrifice his pride during therapy sessions, and he did it with pure, untainted love.

And my mother. In the beginning she was my trusted confidant and guide to the world; I remember being in first grade and her sitting with me on the stairs, explaining how to stand up to a bully. And then she was my enemy, the person who could never know the truth—no matter the circumstances. She saw me at my absolute worst and still tried to pull me out of the dark hole I was living in. Now I think of her as a mentor. She gives me advice and leaves it up to me to follow it. She has stopped looking for deception, and I have stopped trying to deceive. Even though the wounds have healed, there are still so many scars. But at least that is all that is left: the scars.

The most important thing to remember is that every day is a new day. Every morning when I wake up is another chance. I love that. I have spent so much time trying to find myself in a tragic mix of low self-esteem, growing pains, and the horror of an eating disorder; and I screwed up—a lot. Lucky for me, I never gave up, and no one ever gave up on me. I finally fought back and learned what a waste of a person I was while the bulimia ruled my life. More importantly, I learned what an amazing person I actually am—all by myself. I turned out okay.

And I am so proud.

EPILOGUE: PART 2

I Hope Your Dreams Come True

Two years have passed since we dropped Taryn off at school. Two years since I sat crying in our car, with my family around me and Taryn's note in my lap. That note was one of affirmation for me. It told me two very important things. First, I knew that she loved me, but this told me she respected all my efforts to help her, and I felt a peace in turning her recovery over to her without any guilt that I should have done more. Second, Taryn, in her own words, said that she was going to turn out alright in the end. She would get better. It might not happen overnight, or even that summer or that year. She might take two steps forward and then one step back. But she was on the path.

Our trust issues remained a problem for a very long time; in fact, Steve and I still have moments when we catch ourselves asking, "Do you think that's true?" Eating disorders, by their very nature, thrive in a deceptive, manipulative atmosphere, and the lies compound into bigger lies, more complicated lies, more dangerous lies. Try as we might, we had been sucked in too many times, and we have had a difficult time leaving ourselves vulnerable to trust again. You can't force yourself to trust—either you do or you don't. Taryn wonders if we will ever trust her, and while I know we will, she knows that has been a sad price to pay.

216

So what can be learned from my family's experiences? How can other parents, spouses, friends, and families of those battling eating disorders gain from our anguish? For one thing, know you are not alone. You are not the only one who does not understand, who is not sure what you can do, and who is scared out of your mind as you watch your loved one slide down the slippery slope. You would be surprised to learn how many of us are out there. When my story became more public, people came out of the woodwork—everyone had a story to tell about their sister, their daughter-in-law, their college roommate; I couldn't believe how common this problem is.

One of my most valuable lessons, and the one I think is the most helpful, was about separating your journey from that of your struggling loved one's. I wanted so much to just fix the problem, but it became excruciatingly frustrating because it wasn't my problem to fix. When I thought about it in those terms, I began to handle it very differently. Her road included a giant eating disorder boulder to navigate, and by overcoming it, and figuring it all out, she would grow and enhance herself as a person.

My road had a different boulder blocking the way. My boulder was that my beloved daughter had an eating disorder. Because of the challenges that particular obstacle presented to me, I learned some of life's biggest lessons. As awful as that time period in my life was, I definitely grew and even gained some wisdom. That was one of the many lessons I eventually absorbed during our terrible eating disorder adventure. It may have been the hard way, but I learned to let go.

Although it may not be for everyone, I received a great deal of comfort from putting my anguish in God's hands. My faith opened my mind to understanding things like letting go, realizing Taryn and I had our own roads to travel, and accepting that there were some things I couldn't change or resolve. It wasn't in my nature to just step back, and through God, I was able to find the strength to put the frustration aside and be patient. It wasn't easy, and I didn't always succeed, but I learned it was what I had to do.

I also realized how important it is to take care of yourself. I was so busy funneling all my energy into trying to help Taryn that I didn't recognize that I was close to the edge myself. Eating disorders don't only hold the target hostage; they hijack the family as well. It's hard to comprehend how consuming the battle against anorexia and bulimia can be for the parent. It's naturally terrible for the patient, but it's also agony for the family. You watch your child, your sister, your spouse deteriorate physically, or you imagine the damage being done; and the enemy is food, something they can't live without. It becomes your focus in life, and you neglect yourself.

I remember a woman who was hospitalized in the facility near our home. She went on many talk shows and soon became known as the 57-pound woman. I wondered where her family was—how could her mother and father let her get to this desperate point? I, like most people, sat in judgment and questioned their parental motives. Now I know—they were probably following advice to let go and take care of themselves, because it was not their battle to win.

Then there was the woman I recently met who could not let go. She was in the area to help her daughter, an anorectic. Her daughter was forty-seven years old. She had three children. She had been suffering since she was fourteen. She weighed eighty-eight pounds, and her mother was frantic to help her. She was trying to be there for her daughter and for her grandchildren. It was all the woman could think about; her life was not her own.

For me, getting informed was a very helpful and therapeutic approach to dealing with what was happening to me—and I do mean happening to me and not just Taryn. I thought I knew all about eating disorders until one consumed my daughter. Through research, phone calls, the Internet, and more, I could at least find options to try, and it helped me to understand much of what was happening.

As a parent, you must do the best that you can, find what you feel comfortable doing, and live with it, because you'll never know what magic trick will stop the disorder. We ended up sending Taryn to two facilities in our desperation, plus several years of therapy, but some parents cannot bear the idea of sending their daughter away. While both parents might feel content with their decisions, rarely will you be 100 percent sure you're doing the right thing. In the end, it will be your daughter who decides to recover, or not to recover, for her own reasons.

The reasons can vary tremendously. I met one woman, Debbie, who confessed that she had struggled with a serious case of anorexia in college. She told me that nothing her parents did worked until they started ignoring the problem. They stopped talking about it, stopped monitoring her, and stopped taking her to therapy; they just acted like it didn't exist. And for her, that was a turning point, the beginning of the end of her anorexia.

My niece was bulimic for a year. She stopped when she saw the damage being done to her teeth. Having nice teeth was more important to her than her bulimia. End of story. As a parent, spouse, friend, or family member, you have to operate within your own comfort zone as you try to offer options and support, because no one knows what bit of information, event, or action will trigger an individual's recovery.

Another important message is that you can't put the weight of the recovery on your own shoulders. I kept worrying that if I made the wrong move or decision, or if I said or did the wrong thing, it would hamper Taryn's healing process. As her mom, I felt a responsibility to rescue her, and I left no rock unturned in my attempts. For me, doing so gave me a peace of mind in the end that I had definitely done everything I could do. However, I wonder. If I'd done nothing, as Debbie's parents did, would it have just gone away?

I like to think that for us, I made the right choice. Of course, a college education's worth of dollars later, I need to think that way. I'll never know for sure. I choose to believe that somewhere along the way, something stuck with Taryn, and if it didn't push her to improve, maybe it helped her once she made the decision. Each person must make their own choice.

So often, parents, and especially mothers, see at least part of their role as the Happy Maker. We kiss the boo-boos; we fix things and make them better. We nurture, comfort, and do what we need to do to make our family happy. We nag, cajole, and encourage our kids to be the best they can be. When your child has an eating disorder, it is a special kind of torment for the mother, who cannot fix this and cannot make her child happy.

It's important for loved ones to know that there is an absolute limit to what you can do to help. Until the affected person decides she wants to change, that recovery is now her idea; it's just not going to happen. Willing it to change won't make it happen, but you can continue to help and try to guide her toward the light through therapy and love. Until she or he wants it, however, and is willing to be truthful, honest, and hardworking, you can only accomplish so much.

Do we regret all the time, money, and effort we put forth before Taryn honestly began her own work? I don't. It would be hard to know for sure whether her first stay in Arizona gave her more ideas on how to hide and luxuriate in her eating disorder, or more valuable information to use when she did finally decide to recover. I tend to think a little of both, but I believe she would have found the tips and tricks on the Internet pro–eating disorder websites anyway. I feel she made valuable progress there, and later in therapy, in figuring out why she jumped headlong into her eating disorder, and she learned that she deserved to value herself. It just took her a long time to figure out how, and she's still working on tweaking that concept. Maybe we all are.

I also learned a major lesson on acceptance. When our children are babies, and even before they are born, we have so many happy expectations. We anticipate their first steps, their first words, their first kisses. We look forward to the milestones in their lives, assuming we'll get choked up as our kindergartner gets on the bus on her first day of school, or when our third grader is in his first play.

We count on our child to be the best at something he or she loves, because in our hearts, they are the best. As we raise our babies, we think we know who they are, but often in our eyes, they are who we want them to be. We see their potential; we imagine who they will become and what they can accomplish.

The point is not "did we push them" or "did we hurry them," because in our society, a parent can hardly help but worry if their youngster has achieved what they need to get into the college of his or her choice. The point is, as they grow up, we have to learn to let go of some of our expectations and accept and appreciate who they really are.

I sang a lullaby to all three of my girls. Just after Taryn was born, I heard a song that I instantly loved, and I wrote down the main verse. Starting with Taryn, I wrote a stanza with each daughter, until the song eventually had four verses.

My Babies' Lullaby

WHERE ARE YOU GOING?
I WISH I KNEW.
OFF TO WHEREVER,
I HOPE YOUR DREAMS COME TRUE.
WHERE IS WHEREVER?
WILL WE EVER KNOW?
HOW WILL I EVER LET YOU GO?

YOU ARE SO SMALL NOW,
BUT BIGGER EACH DAY.
TIME GOES SO QUICKLY,
THE MONTHS JUST PASS AWAY.
SOON YOU'LL BE RUNNING,
THEN OUT ON YOUR OWN.
WHERE DID THE YEARS GO?
NOW YOU'RE GROWN.

BABIES GROW QUICKLY
TOO QUICKLY IT SEEMS
ONE DAY THEY'RE CRAWLING,
THEN REACHING FOR THEIR DREAMS.
WHAT ARE YOUR DREAMS?
AND WILL THEY ALL COME TRUE?
WE'LL BE HERE WATCHING.
OUR DREAM WAS YOU.

MOMMA LOVES YOU
DADDY DOES TOO
WE KNOW YOU'RE PRECIOUS
YOU KNOW WE'RE HERE FOR YOU.
YOU ARE OUR BABY
AND YOU'LL ALWAYS BE.
EVEN WHEN YOU
TURN TWENTY-THREE.

In retrospect, I realize that ironically, the lullaby speaks exactly to this idea of appreciating who your child is rather than who you expect him or her to be. It speaks to the quick passage of time; from holding your tiny infant, and then in the blink of an eye, watching with love as they pursue their dreams and goals—not yours.

You would think, writing these words, and singing them nightly for so many years, that I might have gotten the message. But it wasn't until I first descended into the hellish nightmare of Taryn's eating disorder, and then found my way to a new level of awareness, that I realized I had to live my lullaby. I had to let her go. And I had to accept that she has her journey, and I have mine.

The good news is that the last verse is also true. She will always be my baby. We made it through a living nightmare, and I will always love her unconditionally. As we travel through our lives, which I'm sure will not be without more challenges, I do believe we will always be there for each other.

Resources

EATING DISORDER TYPES AND SYMPTOMS

Anorexia Nervosa
- Significant weight loss (15% below normal weight for height)
- Refusal to maintain a normal weight for one's height, body type, age, and activity level
- Continual dieting despite being underweight
- Fear of gaining weight and becoming fat
- Inaccurate perception of one's body, such as feeling fat despite being underweight
- Amenorrhea (loss of menstrual period) in females
- Compulsive exercise

Bulimia Nervosa
- Frequent binges, or the uncontrolled, impulsive consumption of a large amount of food in a short period of time
- Purging behaviors following binges including self-induced vomiting, abuse of laxatives, diuretics, or diet pills, fasting, excessive exercise
- Preoccupation with food and weight
- Feelings of shame about the bingeing and purging

Binge Eating Disorder
- Frequent binges without purging behaviors
- Feelings of shame and self-hatred about the bingeing
- Often accompanied by excessive weight gain and obesity

Eating Disorders Not Otherwise Specified (EDNOS)

- Other disordered eating patterns don't fit into the other types of eating disorders or don't have all of the characteristics of a full-fledged eating disorder
- Chewing food and spitting it out without swallowing

WARNING SIGNS OF EATING DISORDERS

- Abnormal preoccupation with body appearance or weight
- Abnormal preoccupation with food, nutrition, calories, health, and/or cooking
- Frequent trips to the bathroom after meals
- Depression and suicidal thoughts
- A significant change in appetite
- Excessive exercise despite fatigue or weakness
- Moodiness and irritability
- Reduced concentration, memory, and thinking ability
- Loss of interest in hobbies and schoolwork
- Anxiety, especially around food and mealtimes
- Feelings of guilt and self-hatred
- Constantly making excuses to avoid eating
- Compulsive rituals surrounding food and meal times, such as not letting different foods touch each other or eating only one type of food at a time
- Wearing excessively baggy or bulky clothes
- Hoarding food
- Isolation and withdrawal from friends
- Complete avoidance of social situations involving food, including family meals
- Significant reduction in food intake
- Denial of hunger
- Strange eating habits such as playing with food instead of eating it
- Constant concern about weight

- Secretiveness and deceitfulness
- Preference to eat in isolation
- Reddened fingers, sores in and around mouth, and swollen cheeks or glands (caused by self-inducing vomiting)
- Obsession with clothing size, scales, and mirrors
- Problems with drugs, alcohol, sexual promiscuity, or crime (especially with bulimia)

OBSESSIVE FOOD BEHAVIORS

- Pulling food apart for consumption
- Cutting food into extremely small pieces
- Eating finger foods with forks (such as sandwiches)
- Eating everything with fingers
- Inappropriate or excessive use of condiments
- Separating or organizing food on plate before eating
- Not allowing different food items to touch each other
- Eating only one food group at a time
- Eating food groups in certain orders
- Inappropriate food mixing
- Eating extremely quickly or slowly
- Not taking eyes off plate
- Refusing to look at plate
- Comparing plate to others
- Covering or hiding food
- Drinking excessive amounts while eating
- Refusing to drink while eating
- Eating condiments by themselves

PHYSICAL PROBLEMS CAUSED BY EATING DISORDERS

- Amenorrhea (loss of menstrual period) or irregular menstruation in females

- Bowel problems, including constipation, diarrhea, bloating, and/or cramps
- Sore throat
- Bursting of blood vessels in eyes (caused by self-induced vomiting)
- Dry skin
- Dry/brittle hair and nails
- Thinning scalp hair
- Dizziness and faintness
- Indigestion and heartburn
- Bruising easily
- Extreme weight loss or rapid fluctuation in weight
- Erosion of tooth enamel and increased cavities and other dental problems
- Fatigue
- Dehydration
- Edema (swelling due to retention in body fluid)
- Sensitivity to the cold
- Reduced metabolic rate
- Slow heart rate
- Irregular heart rhythms
- Shakiness
- Confusion and irritability
- Low blood pressure and high pulse deficit
- Electrolyte imbalances
- Reduced body temperature, which can cause bluish-colored extremities
- Hypoglycemia (low blood glucose levels)
- Coma
- Chronic kidney problems
- Irritation and tears in the esophagus
- Low potassium
- Insomnia
- Growth of lanugo (fine hair on body surface)
- Mortality rate is 5–15%

EATING DISORDER FACILITIES

The authors are not recommending or endorsing these facilities, associations, or websites. This list is for information only.

CENTER FOR DISCOVERY

www.centerfordiscovery.com, 800-760-3934, 562-425-6404
4136 Ann Arbor Rd., Lakewood, CA 90712

THE EATING DISORDER CENTER AT ROGERS MEMORIAL HOSPITAL

www.rogershospital.org, 1-800-767-4411
34700 Valley Rd., Oconomowac, WI 53066

FAIRWINDS

www.fairwindstreatment.com, 727-449-0300, 800-225-0301
1569 S. Ft. Harrison Ave., Clearwater, FL 33756

LAUREATE PSYCHIATRIC CLINIC AND HOSPITAL

www.laureate.com, 918-491-5600
6655 S. Yale Ave., Tulsa, OK 74136

MERCY MINISTRIES

www.mercyministries.org, 615-831-6987
15328 Old Hickory Blvd., Nashville, TN 37211

REMUDA RANCH

www.remudaranch.com, 1-800-445-1900, 928-684-3913
One East Apache Street, Wickenburg, AZ 85390

RENFREW CENTER

www.renfrew.org, www.renfrewcenter.com, 1-800-RENFREW

EATING DISORDER ASSOCIATIONS

NATIONAL EATING DISORDERS ASSOCIATION

www.edap.org, 206-382-3587
603 Stewart St. Suite 803, Seattle, WA 98101

NATIONAL ASSOCIATION OF ANOREXIA NERVOSA AND OTHER ASSOCIATED DISORDERS

www.anad.org, 847-433-3996 or 847-831-3438
P.O. Box 7, Highland Park, IL 60035

OTHER INFORMATIONAL WEBSITES

www.something-fishy.org/
www.mirror-mirror.org/eatdis.htm